RAIDERS OF THE 'FREE LAND'

Fr.

My Khyber Marriage

by
Morag Murray Abdullah

The Long Riders' Guild Press
www.thelongridersguild.com
ISBN No: 1-59048-087-2

To the Reader:

The editors and publishers of The Long Riders' Guild Press faced significant technical and financial difficulties in bringing this and the other titles in the Equestrian Travel Classics collection to the light of day.

Though the authors represented in this international series envisioned their stories being shared for generations to come, all too often that was not the case. Sadly, many of the books now being published by The Long Riders' Guild Press were discovered gracing the bookshelves of rare book dealers, adorned with princely prices that placed them out of financial reach of the common reader. The remainder were found lying neglected on the scrap heap of history, their once-proud stories forgotten, their once-glorious covers stained by the toil of time and a host of indifferent previous owners.

However The Long Riders' Guild Press passionately believes that this book, and its literary sisters, remain of global interest and importance. We stand committed, therefore, to bringing our readers the best copy of these classics at the most affordable price. The copy which you now hold may have small blemishes originating from the master text.

We apologize in advance for any defects of this nature.

CONTENTS

ILLUSTRATIONS

CHAPTER I

THE HILL CHIEFTAIN'S SON

THE War raged on. It was 1916. Trainloads of troops kept leaving. The streets of Edinburgh were full of wounded men. Everybody was doing something, some war work. Up till then I had spent my time painting, but I felt anxious to get away from this solitary occupation and mix with people who might help me to forget the shock of my brother's death in France. A friend suggested I might do voluntary work at the bandage and sphagnum moss *dépôt*, or at the flag *dépôt*. I chose the latter, and worked hard getting boxes and flags ready for hundreds of sellers, and then sold flags myself from 5.30 A.M. until after 6 at night.

It was during one of these flag days that a lady in charge of a *dépôt* invited me to a reception at the University. All the voluntary flag-sellers were to go. My father gave his views on the affair and was not flattering in his remarks about the 'wild students' I should meet there. In the end my pleading was successful, and he agreed to my going provided I reached home no later than ten o'clock. This meant I should have only two hours there, but, having been to so few entertainments of the kind, I was tremendously excited.

At last the day came. I had spent all my available

spare time choosing a frock of pink taffeta, pink shoes and stockings, and a double row of pink moss-roses for my hair. On my arrival the Professors were receiving. I felt lost among so many students and wished I had never come. The lady who had invited me came to speak to me, introduced me to a girl student, then left us together. There were all nationalities—tiny Japs, gigantic Zulus, sleek-headed Indians, and innumerable girls. I watched them all arriving. It amused me to see how nervous some of them felt, and caused me to feel a little more at ease. The big room was becoming full and the guests ranged themselves nearer to the walls. Suddenly an Eastern student appeared at the entrance. His appearance was different from the others. I could not think what his nationality might be and asked my companion.

"Oh, that is Syed Abdullah. I believe he's the son of an Indian Frontier chieftain. He's terribly clever. Would you like to meet him? I know him well."

Seeing and meeting seemed a different thing, however, and I said nervously, "Not just now." Nevertheless I followed the chieftain's son with my eyes as he crossed the room. He walked so erectly and looked like the popular idea of a handsome sheikh. He was tall, with finely chiselled features and the air of a swashbuckler, yet there was no 'side' about him. I could tell that his bearing was natural. He seemed defiant and yet devil-may-care, and I could look at no one else. To me he was the principal actor on the stage. How delightfully he bowed, I thought, to the women there. Why had it not been my luck to be one of them and to be in that particular corner? Yet, on the other hand, I felt glad to be half-hidden where it was possible to see him. He glanced round the room as a conqueror might have surveyed the legions he had captured, but there was nothing insolent in the gaze. It was not for anyone in particular.

He was coming our way now! "There he is!" I said excitedly to my student companion, while my confusion was almost overpowering. Too late I whispered to her, "Don't ask him to come"; she was already speaking to him, while he bowed again in that inimitable way of his. They were now beside me, but I continued to hide behind some guests and the girl had to pull me out.

"Meet my fellow-student, Syed Abdullah. This is Morag Murray." He was now bowing to me, while I, faced with the only person I wanted to meet in the room, felt suddenly too shy to look at him and heartily wished the ground would swallow me up. The girl now left us together, and my new companion asked whether he might bring me some tea.

I felt it must all be a dream—the likelihood of my being allowed to attend a reception at the University, and now to be waited upon by such a cavalier! Syed Abdullah returned with a cup of tea and some chocolate cake. I found my tongue and thanked him, asking why he had not brought any for himself.

"In my hills we drink only green tea and do not like this black tea. Moreover, we are men of the sword and do not care for sugar buns."

How marvellously he spoke! "Men of the hills," he had said. Then I would talk to him of the hills I loved too; he would understand. So we talked of my hills and of his, until suddenly, like Cinderella, I discovered it was 10.30 P.M. I had promised my father to be home at ten, and on this, really my first, outing I had broken my promise!

Fear seized me. "Oh!" I gasped. "I ought to have been home by now. My father will be angry. What shall I do? It's now ten-thirty and I have some distance to go home."

"Where do you live?"

I told him, already almost weeping.

"Perhaps I may take you home in my car with your chaperon?"

I could not find my chaperon anywhere and perhaps was not too anxious to. In any case, within the next few minutes Syed Abdullah and I were sitting in the little car speeding towards my home. My thoughts meanwhile were torn between the bliss of being alone with such a wonderful companion and the fear of my father seeing me arrive back with an unknown young man—and at that late hour.

I got out quickly and my companion stood beside me. Fearful lest I might be seen by my father, I hurriedly said, "Good night and thank you!"

"Good night. I hope to have the pleasure of meeting you again," replied Syed Abdullah as he kissed my hand. I am afraid even the street lamps showed only too plainly that we were unwilling to part.

"My father would not allow us to meet again," I said disappointedly and ran up the few steps to the door. As I opened it I looked once again at my escort, who was standing on the pavement. I quickly closed the door and thought about nothing but the way Syed Abdullah had looked at me, spoken to me, and attended to me, until I went to sleep.

Next morning I awoke late to find a letter awaiting me. It ran:

> Please, Morag, do me the kindness of having tea with me this afternoon at Mackie's at 4 o'clock.
>
> SYED ABDULLAH

I was so delighted at the prospect of seeing my cavalier so soon that the day seemed never to pass. Telling my parents I was going to tea with a friend of the family I left an hour before the time, so afraid was I of being late, although it was only a few minutes' walk to reach the café.

By 3.30 Syed Abdullah arrived, and I suddenly became silent. We sat at a window-table looking over Princes Street gardens. By and by I told him of the old home we had left the year before, of my pets in the country—and about my brother.

"I am so sorry for you, poor child," he said so comfortingly that the sympathy made me cry. He changed the subject and told me about his home, a fort in the 'no man's land' of the Khyber Pass, and I became so interested in hearing about his clansmen that my sorrow was forgotten. When he told me of the fighting men at home his eyes became almost gripping in their intensity; next moment, with eyes as soft as a woman's, he was telling me of his mother and sisters.

The time passed so quickly, like all happy times, that it was late before we realized it.

"Is it really five o'clock?" said my companion, and I felt glad he had not thought the time long.

We met nearly every day after that—went to the Braid Hills to golf, had tea at the hotel there, and were ridiculously happy. Yet this man, although always anxious to see me and seemingly happy when we were together, never kissed me and spoke only of everyday things. When we parted he raised my hand to his lips. He did not now seem like the Eastern sheikhs at the cinema! He said none of the things the picture hero had said, and did not tell me whether he even liked me, although his attitude was always so kind and protective that I felt he must, or why should he want to see me so often?

About this time, a few months after we first met, my father told me he wanted to speak to me.

The son of a boyhood friend of his, he said, was coming home from France, and the two fathers thought that as we got on so well together we might become engaged and be married when the War was over.

I replied that I did not want to become engaged to Roy and that I did not want to marry him.

Whether my father had any knowledge of Syed Abdullah and wanted to be diplomatic about it I do not know; if so, he hid it very well. I told him about my student friend. He listened until the whole story was out, then very determinedly said: "Morag, this friendship must cease. I forbid you to see this Eastern student again, and I shall certainly communicate with the University authorities if I find any disobedience on your part. Sit down now and write a letter I shall dictate to you."

I sat down and wrote the following as instructed by my father as he paced up and down the room:

> SYED ABDULLAH,
>
> I shall not be able to see you again and hope you will not make any effort to see me. I am about to become engaged to be married and in these circumstances you will understand our meetings must cease.
>
> MORAG MURRAY

My father went to post the letter himself. I was too stunned to cry. All the old misery came back. Yesterday I was happy, to-day in the depths of despair.

That night I begged my father to ask Syed Abdullah to come to talk to him.

His 'word,' he said, was final, and in view of the recent sorrow we had sustained he hoped I would not distress him and my mother by any disobedience.

The following day Roy arrived in Edinburgh. He had been in hospital and was given ten days' home leave. Naturally I was glad to welcome a War hero, but I could think of no one but Syed Abdullah. What would he think of me? How mean I should appear!

I could not bear the suspense and parting, and

wrote telling him the letter had been written under my father's direction, and that I did want to see him soon.

A reply came by special messenger the same evening to say he was waiting to see me in the Caledonian Station. Not a very romantic setting!

Hurriedly putting on my coat and hat I ran all the way and arrived to find him waiting. I wanted to throw my arms round his neck, so relieved was I to see him, but he looked so sadly at me that I felt something terrible must have happened since we parted.

"Morag," he said, "I thought you were not coming. I have missed seeing you."

"And I have missed you," I said.

"My car is outside. Let us go to the Braid Hills and talk."

We did not speak until we were actually on the hills. Syed Abdullah was in deep thought.

"Your letter," he began, "was a great surprise to me. If you had told me before I should not have been so distressed."

"I had to write it, my father was so angry," I protested.

"I want you to understand that we—that is, my clan—look upon our women with the greatest respect. The care we lavish on them and our anxiety to protect them from any harm has gained for us the reputation of making slaves of them. That is not the case. We reverence them, and the worst crime in my hills is abduction. I have no wish to claim another man's bride. Such a thing at home would cause clan warfare which would not stop until every male member of the offending one's clan had been wiped out."

"But there's no reason for you to think like this. I'm not engaged to anyone—my father and a friend have set their minds upon this marriage, that is all. I shall not marry Roy Graham. I don't like him well enough."

"Morag, is there any man, any one of your own countrymen you would marry?"

"No," I replied.

"Then you will not have to obey your father and marry some one of his choice?"

"No."

"Then as you are free I want to tell you I love you—ever since I saw you at the reception—and I always shall love you. If I get my father's permission, and your father's, will you marry me?"

"Yes," I replied.

We stood for long that afternoon, too deliciously happy to part.

Next day we met and discussed Syed Abdullah's visit to my father. Roy was going back to France next day, and we arranged for the visit to be on the day following. My mother was quite pleased when I asked whether my friend might come to tea; as she had agreed, I left it to her to break it to Father. The day came, and tea-time brought Syed Abdullah. My mother was delighted with him, but my father in their talk after tea told him that I was too young to marry and looked older than I was, and he would not give his consent.

Syed Abdullah cabled to his father. The reply was short: "Positively not."

Syed and I were distracted between the two fathers. Another cable came to say, "Important letter follows." This arrived weeks later. In it the Chieftain said he was then thinking of negotiating a marriage between Syed Abdullah and the daughter of a powerful rival chieftain and that once it was arranged it was irrevocable—for in the Pathan country an engagement must never on any account be broken. He also pointed out that I was not of the Muslim faith, and he asked whether I came of a Highland clan of warriors and whether I was able to hold the fort if called upon.

Syed cabled back that I belonged to a Highland clan and was willing to become Muslim, and he took it upon himself to vouch for my ability to guard any fort!

The reply said: "If you two are sure of your ability to remain faithful for life to each other, marry by both Eastern and Western law, and afterwards marry here in the ancient stronghold of your ancestors. Blessings upon you both! May Allah keep you! This is my permission."

CHAPTER II

TO 'NO MAN'S LAND'

THE cable with the Chieftain's consent set our minds at ease, but my father refused to consider our engagement, and all day and until late at night my life was one long-drawn-out repetition of stories of girls who had married Orientals only to find on the first visit to their husband's country that he was already married, perhaps more than once, and that the new bride was obliged to wait hand and foot on the relations and finally, having been starved or deserted, was obliged to throw herself on a missionary's mercy. There were wild tales of British girls having been killed mysteriously and never heard of again. I was told that all Orientals were married in their cradles and that it was a ninety-nine-per-cent. possibility that Syed Abdullah was married and that once in his country he would return to the degenerate ways of his clan and I would either be given ground glass in my food or be made a slave to his relations, whose womenfolk would be madly jealous of me.

I felt ashamed to tell Syed these things at first, but determined to give him the chance of contradicting them. He was quite aware of what the Western opinion was and told me that most of the tales were carried by women who had married

Orientals thinking them to be princes and looking forward to a life of luxury in some Aladdin-like palace of their own imagination, and, when they found out that there were neither princes nor palaces in their new lives, 'went gay' with the probably rather sketchy European population who could be persuaded to 'go gay' with them, and finally, if lucky and still unashamed, they had found their disillusioned way home. Moreover, people assured me that Orientals lived in mud huts, were half clad, heathen, and no better than wild savages.

Syed, on his side, was told by his compatriots of the mistake of taking a Western wife. They said all Western women were the same—waited until they got out East and then danced and drank with their own people; flirted with other women's husbands and generally became impossible to live with; and then, returning home, wrote lurid stories that editors were only too glad to print.

Syed stressed the point that the Khyber men were not Indians, and after learning about his home life I was quite willing to share it. My aunt alleged she had had two weak turns and several fainting fits since hearing the news, and descended upon me escorted by her Scrooge-like lawyer, who showed me her will in which everything she possessed in this world, and all the prayers she would have power to offer for me in the next, were mine if I would marry the man my father had chosen for me. She did not want a reply, but thought the longing to possess her future wealth would outweigh a very uncertain future in foreign hills where every man had at least four wives!

Every day for a week she and the lawyer came to see me. I refused to listen to her persuasions, whereupon she finally drew up a new will to which my father and mother were witnesses. In this will she left everything to a home for strayed cats.

When my father saw I was not to be influenced he grudgingly allowed Syed Abdullah to come to our house. They became very good friends and within three months of our meeting we were married. Three prominent Muslims who were then in Edinburgh came to my home, and the ceremony—a very simple one—took place in our drawing-room. One acted as priest, the other two as witnesses. I was asked thrice the same question:

"Do you take this man Syed Abdullah, son of Chieftain Secunder Khan, as your husband, and do you accept a thousand pounds as your dowry?"

Then it was Syed's turn:

"Do you take this woman, Morag Murray, the daughter of James Murray, as your wife, and do you agree to pay one thousand pounds as dowry to her at any time she may demand it during your lifetime, or, should she not demand it, do you agree that it be the first claim paid from your estate after your death?"

Three times the question was put and three times answered in the affirmative.

The two witnesses were now asked whether they had heard the parties agree to the contract, and whether they were willing to witness. The reading of a chapter of the Koran in which the contracting parties are enjoined to respect the marriage agreement, and to live with respect and devotion towards each other, was followed by the drawing up of terms of agreement. My husband, myself, the priest, and both witnesses appended signatures. The ceremony was over. It had been solemnized strictly in accordance with Muslim laws, since I had previously embraced the Muslim faith with its simple belief in the unity of God and the prophethood of Mohammed.

The following year a daughter was born to us. The event occurred during the awful influenza epidemic, when my husband was in a nursing-home just recovering from the disease. Thinking to cheer him up, my father sent the good news to him. That night at 12 o'clock my nurse thought she heard some one outside the front door. Opening it she found a man huddled up on the doorstep, soaked through and wearing nothing but pyjamas and a dressing-gown. It was Syed, who had run away when told he was not well enough to leave! The exertion of the four-mile walk had been too much for his strength. He remained unconscious for several hours, and had a relapse from which he almost died.

Shortly after this the Armistice came. The bells and sirens did not bring to some of us the joy that others felt, but it was certainly a relief, and in the first rush of new freedom we vowed to be better than we had ever been before!

Some well-meaning friends had told me that my

'in-laws' would not care for the child (being a girl) and that it would be better not to inform them of her birth; they assured me that only boys were welcome "anywhere in the East."

Judging his family's reaction by my husband's, however, I cabled the news, and to my infinite relief received this answer: "The Chief of the Clan and all the members thereof send their blessings on the arrival of the little one. May the blessing of Allah be with you too! We desire to celebrate the occasion in these hills and are preparing for your coming. Peace be with you!"

A letter came next asking us to leave as soon as possible. But to undertake the long fatiguing journey with so young a child was too great a problem for us, and our war-shattered nerves and half-starved bodies made a rest imperative after the influenza. It was not till two and a half years later that we left for the Khyber.

The journey to Karachi was an ordinary sea-trip. Karachi itself is a strange mixture of East and West—great camels jostling with up-to-date cars, and taxi-drivers bargaining to show one the sights "with English-speaking guides," the latter being sometimes not more than ten years old and dressed in "European style," which comprises sandals, an ancient bowler-hat several sizes too big, and a head-to-foot garment which might be a converted flour-bag. We were begged to buy ivory beads and bracelets, golden Buddhas, embroideries and carpets, by wily shopkeepers who knew greenhorns when they saw them and were determined to make the most while their luck was in. They would start the price at, say, fifty rupees, and end by saying that if we kept quiet we could have the object for five rupees—probably double its real worth.

The would-be guides call Western women either "Mrs McGregor" or "Mrs Lloyd George" and can speak English very well. The taxi-drivers care neither for life nor law. Our taxi ran over a dog before we had gone a hundred yards. I begged the driver to stop, but he seemed to have become suddenly deaf. He swerved past a loaded camel and almost deposited us in the centre of a villagers' council by the wayside. We drew up with a bump, and fearing we would be arrested I tried to join in the conversation between the driver and the head elder of the village, but to no avail. The interpreter-guide said the taxi-man was telling the villagers in Hindustani that they were but a pollution under the feet of the great English lady who owned nearly all the lands over the ocean and could have them put directly into the sea if she chose! At this they all put their faces to the ground and—the guide said—called upon Allah to protect them from my wrath. To hide my amusement I was obliged to lower my head so that my sun-helmet hid my laughter. This they took to mean my royal dispensation in their favour and they proceeded to kiss the taxi-door in gratitude.

When we reached our hotel the taxi-driver, in spite of his manœuvres in all directions, was delighted with a rupee tip (1*s.* 4*d.*). He said he would not do any work for the next ten days, and insisted upon seeing us safely into the train for Peshawar. By the time the train left the taxi-driver had gathered what looked like his whole clan with the object of selling fruit, nuts, sweets, and soft drinks. Each time any money was paid to them we noticed that something was handed to the taxi-man, who probably made more out of the 'introduction' than he would have earned in a week.

My Scottish nurse left us at Karachi and I engaged an Indian hill-woman who had good references from a former employer.

The journey took two days, but luckily the weather was cool. After we crossed the Indus the country changed and we began to see a different type of men—tall, fairer-complexioned, dressed in baggy trousers and embroidered waistcoats, with loose shirts hanging outside the trousers, and turbans.

Near Peshawar men were ploughing with rifles slung over their shoulders. As the train entered the barbed-wire-encircled station tall Pathan Guards (Military Police) boarded the train to see our papers. It was as though we had entered a war area and were suspects—as indeed every one is until he has proved his identity.

Having satisfied the Military Police that we had not arrived to lay siege to the place, we drove to the town house of the Chieftain. From the outside this looked none too welcoming. Grim walls, loop-holed, frowned down upon us, but once inside we were very comfortable.

I was anxious the next day to see more of the bazaar (the streets of shops in the city) and decided the best way to do this was to put on a *burka*. This garment, worn by all Muslim women outside their homes, is a combined hood and cloak, yards wide round the skirt, reaching the ground; through two eyelet-holes covered with net one sees all that is going on. All women look alike in this white enveloping garment and at first, until one becomes accustomed to it, it gives one the feeling of being and looking like an apparition.

Peshawar has wide streets, kept wonderfully clean. Procession of camels from Central Asia laden with every kind of merchandise lumber through the streets. Huge tall men, wearing big turbans tied jauntily, stride past, and their baggy trousers tight round the ankles and gaily embroidered coats lend an Ali-Baba-like air to the place. Groups of them squat in the open-air booths drinking green tea and chewing walnuts and dried mulberries. Their black bobbed hair curls round the edges of their turbans. All have dark flashing eyes, fine features, and hooked noses. The little open-fronted shops, with the owners sitting placidly in front, contain a miscellaneous assortment of melons, sweets, nuts, brass-ware, sandals, etc. Shopkeeping is a leisurely occupation, and the greatest effort in connexion with it seems to be saluting the passers-by. Over the streets are the verandas where the more complicated trade of drug-vending takes place. These drugs provide the most highly coloured foretaste of what the hereafter is supposed to be and a speedy way of attaining it.

After two days' rest we left Peshawar by road

THE KHYBER PASS

through the Khyber Pass. The great rocks, towering boulder upon boulder to heights ranging from 600 to 1000 feet, strike a peculiar terror in the traveller. In some places the pass is so narrow that four camels cannot walk abreast. At the actual frontier there is a 'turnstile' through which one passes into 'No Man's Land.' That turnstile looks unimportant. It should be massive and stand for what it is, the gate leading to what is one of the least known and most remarkable countries in the world—a strip of land neither Indian nor Afghan, inhabited by clans who owe allegiance to none but their own chiefs, and live in loopholed towers, always armed and sleeping with their rifles at their sides.

Into this land of mystery I passed through the insignificant turnstile. Certainly I must confess I felt a little the truth of what I had been told in far-away Edinburgh. I stood for a few seconds in wonderment at it all. Was it a dream? Would I awake to find myself in Edinburgh again? I looked back at the last outpost of my own people and knew there would be no possibility of my return if the odds went against me. It is a moment I do not wish anyone to experience, unless they are certain of their ability to face confidently what lies over those hills.

My husband I think sensed my feelings. "Welcome," he said, "to the land of my fathers."

It broke the spell. It reassured me. "Syed," I said, "I trust you. You realize I am friendless here and have only you."

"You and I are together always, Morag," he

answered. "So long as I live I promise to protect you with my life."

Thus we started on our journey. As we passed finally out of sight of the last British post Syed said, "There is still time to go back if you regret your decision. Time for *us* to go back."

"We are not going back," I replied; "at least not yet."

CHAPTER III

MEALS AND PRAYERS WITH THE HILL-MEN

IT is one thing to read about the land beyond the Khyber and another to be actually in it. Compared to it the grim Khyber Pass seemed friendly. Here I felt at the mercy of anything that might be lurking behind those grisly boulders. It was as though I had left something behind at that turnstile; I could only hope it was not courage! Certainly there was no welcome in the bare hills themselves. But we had not much time for meditation, for we were soon met by a party of my husband's clansmen who had been sent to greet us as soon as we were fairly into the 'Free Land of the Hills'—as they style it.

They were all young men, tall, lithe, straight. They embraced my husband, bade us both welcome, and fired a volley in the air, calling in their melodious Pushtu, "Welcome to the land of the free. Welcome to the wife of our noble Chief's son." It reminded me of the ceremony I had witnessed at home when the Freedom of the City of Edinburgh was conferred upon some notable, except that there had been no firing then. These men went ahead of us to clear the road, so to speak, while our ponies made their way slowly behind. The terrors of which I had heard and read in the now almost unbelievable homeland seemed far enough away. Even if any courage had been needed one could depend upon these stalwart leaders to provide it.

On we went, the hills seemed never-ending. Never had I imagined mountains like these. On and on until it was time to stop for refreshment. It was difficult enough to imagine where one would be able to get food, until just round the corner we came upon the house of a khan. One requires to be sure of hospitality when one's party numbers thirty, and it was with not a few misgivings that I saw we were about to throw ourselves upon the kindness of the Khan. As we approached the walled fort—about thirty miles distant from my father-in-law's—the sentries challenged us. "Friends or foes?" "Friends, and peace be upon you!" our men replied. "Welcome, and peace be upon you too!" heartily (and probably with relief) responded the sentries. The gate opened, and our guards stood back while our ponies entered, then came immediately behind us and closed the gate. Two sentries, I noticed as we dismounted, were on guard at the gate.

The Khan, a huge jolly stout man, armed, and dressed in baggy trousers, long embroidered coat, and a tremendous turban, gave us a real Highland welcome. It was not a time when one wanted to receive an address of any length, but it was the correct thing here, and the old Khan was a master at receiving people in the proper manner. A woman servant came and carried Margaret, our little daughter, while two others asked me to follow them. We crossed the courtyard and entered the house. Here another welcome awaited us, and Margaret and I were taken to the women's apartments, whilst Syed stayed outside. These rooms were thick-walled with small windows. The floors were spread with Persian and Bokharan carpets, and against the bare whitewashed walls immense bolster-like cushions rested. We were evidently in the sitting-room of the family. The absence of pictures, ornaments, and furniture gave me a feeling of restful content. I removed my *burka* and breathed a sigh of relief as we sat on the great bolsters. The women of the household, consisting of the Khan's wife and three grown-up daughters, had never seen a Western woman before, and were obviously delighted. They gathered round me, the maidservants in the background, examined my clothes, wound my watch, and would not be happy until I showed them everything I wore! They asked the price, and talked so much and so quickly that the little Pushtu I knew deserted me, and I sat silent and almost overwhelmed. Margaret was playing happily with one of the daughters, and making her own language. Peeping out of the window I saw the men were praying, kneeling on their carpets with their faces turned in the direction of the Holy City of Mecca.

The maid now placed a large white cloth on the carpet in the centre of the floor, and on spotlessly clean tin plates we were given huge helpings of deliciously cooked rice—such as we never see at home—and little discs of roasted meat. The men evidently ate apart. With the name of Allah on our lips we seated ourselves cross-legged on the carpet and ate with our fingers. Margaret asked for a spoon which luckily I had with me, and without further *contretemps* I had my first meal in the 'Free Land.' I noted it was not etiquette to speak or look at anyone during the meal and felt grateful for such a desirable point of table manners.

Two fat-tailed lambs were killed in honour of our visit, and distributed in pieces to the poor dependants of the Khan, and then, to ward off the evil eye, a bowl of linseed oil was brought and a silver cup. I had to dip my little finger into the oil, which was then taken to my husband, who was having food with the men. The bowl was brought again and I dropped a gold coin into it—scarce enough at that time. Knowing what was expected of us, Syed had luckily brought the necessary coins. Both oil and coins were given to the poor at once. The first needy wayfarer who passed was handed the bowl. The women were so delighted to have me that they could not disguise their disappointment when we had to leave. Again they tenderly fingered all my clothes, and gave me gold slippers as a parting gift, making me promise that any time I passed I would be sure to "bring light to their household" by my presence. Donning my *burka* again I joined our party with my daughter. The women chattered like magpies behind the latticed wall, and the Khan gave us a great send-off, thanked us for the great honour we had done him by coming, and ordered ten of his men to see us well on our way. Finally he presented us with two beautiful chargers, exquisitely saddled. Large tassels hung from their ears and silver crescents from the blinkers, while a broad red band encircled their necks. Tassels hung also from the saddles, and the bridles had many tiny jingling bells. This equipment had been presented, the Khan told us, to his father by the Amir of Bokhara. It looked to me as good as new and must have been kept carefully as only people who have few treasures know how to care for them. As I mounted I longed for the old freedom with neither saddle nor *burka*, but I was obliged to follow the custom of the country.

Our escort was worthy of an emperor. Knives and guns dangled from them, and I wondered when these arms would be required in this land of seeming hospitality and remote aloofness. It was not to be long before my enlightenment! It was the duty of this smaller chief to protect us against the warring clansmen in his part of the country, and the guards were an indication of the fact that we were important travellers.

Off we went; our men called back messages of peace and farewell which echoed in the distant hills, and our second welcome was over.

I now began to take stock of our cavaliers. Even the greatest coward might have felt himself safe when surrounded by them. Some wore big fur coats fastened with silver belts over their embroidered waistcoats. Each man carried a rifle slung on his back, a long knife at his belt, and a cartridge-filled bandolier across his chest. They were taking no risks! Their black hair was bobbed, and most of them had beards that did not disguise their youth. Each man looked a trained and fearless warrior. They reminded me of eagles. Two of them played wild warlike chants on reed flutes, others beat small drums as our procession passed from deep gully to deep gully of the parched hills. At one time we were amongst great boulders; at another we were passing through scrub woods with scarcely any visible vegetation—a partridge would start up into the air, or a hare dart away, roused to sudden anxiety by the noise of our party. Then the reed flute and the drums ceased, and there was a deep silence broken by our horses' hooves echoing slightly in the rocks as they struck a stone. It began to feel unreal. A few days ago we had sat in the hotel in Karachi, discussing with our neighbours at the table German submarines, Zeppelins, the plight of the war-distressed countries, and the blessings of being able once more to have a square meal. What did it all matter here? Nothing. The change from the warmth of Karachi to the cold bleakness of these hills was unbelievable. We might have been on another planet.

After a few hours we felt hungry in spite of the food our good friend the Khan had thought worthy of us! We alighted for a meal. Being a woman I was allowed to sit where I liked. It looked as though this meal were going to be a lengthy business. A rough fireplace was constructed and a wood fire made and lighted. Newly killed fat-tailed sheep were roasted whole in their skins on the improvised camp-fire in an incredibly short time. Tin plates appeared from the luggage. Rice was juggled in some marvellous way in the gravy. For the first time in my life I witnessed the great unity of the clans, among whom, according to Muslim law, at meal-time, in war-time, and at prayer-time all men are equal. I was bewildered. I might have been seeing a film in a comfortable cinema. It may have been hunger, it may have been unfamiliarity, but until that day I had never tasted such delicious meat. Savoury and juicy, done to a turn, it had a distinct flavour almost like the nutty taste of really fresh country butter. The meal proceeded in silence, for it is considered bad manners to speak after the name of God is uttered in the grace until one can thank Him again for having given such good food and the health to eat it. Not once did any of these men turn his head to look in my direction. I was their guest and could sit quite comfortably with my *burka* turned back, without being stared at. It was another new experience and one which made the very unaccustomedness delightful. There was not much of the sheep left when we had finished. It might well have been a competition in eating, and a close one! The simplicity of that meal made me decide that tables, chairs, table linen, and cutlery were an unnecessary luxury.

My husband, being the honoured guest, gave the cue for the end of the meal. It was understood by all that when he finished all must finish. He was obliged here to give the others a handicap, for his appetite was not equal to that of the clansmen. He therefore took as long as possible over his food, for it is also etiquette to see that a guest's plate is never empty. It amused me to see Syed eyeing the other heaped plates. I could imagine what was passing through his mind—whether he could continue eating until they finished! Nevertheless, slowly as he ate, he was finished before the others, and he began to nibble a crust of bread. The rest of the clansmen at once stopped and took crusts too. I did exactly as they did. Our crusts were eaten, two men poured water from goat-skins over our hands, my husband now raised his hands, then turning the palms upward he slowly repeated a prayer of thanks to Allah, the Giver of all good. The men folded their hands over their faces and repeated their thanks to the one God "Who brought kindness and food and peace to all."

The feast was over—the most simple, moving, and thrilling one I had ever shared in. We rose from our carpets, for all Muslims carry their carpets with them on such treks, and drank water—this is done only when the meal is finished. Mounting our horses we started again in and out of the winding passes. Some of the defiles were indescribably bleak and inhospitable, and I could easily have believed that any of them led to the lair of a brigand. Now we passed out of the high-walled pass, to be spellbound by the depth of the gullies round the corner. Stones knocked over fell down, down, down, striking less and less loudly against out-jutting rocks. Now we came to the rocks again.

Our next halt was for prayer. Muslims must pray five times daily. My husband led the prayer, I joined in. One needed prayer in this bleak country.

So-called civilization being left behind, one thought more of the Creator of it all, and felt thankful for such blessings as health and strength and safety. We knelt on our carpets with our faces towards Holy Mecca, and thanked God in all simplicity and reverence and sincerity for our safe-conduct so far. This religion gave me a new feeling. There was no pealing organ, no bag in which we had to deposit whatever coin we could most easily silence our conscience with, no wondering whether our clothes were passing muster with the occupants of the seats behind. This was the simplicity of prayer which made it the powerful thing it was. Beside me knelt a mule-driver. At that moment we were both equal, for prayer here humbled my usual conservative ideas of caste and position; yet later on the mule-driver resumed his old status without taking any advantage of the level to which prayer had raised him.

Again we started. I at least was tired, but was only dimly aware of it.

From time to time we saw little forts of clansmen who lived in a state of perpetual war with each other. Some ancient feud made life a precious commodity. Men who pursued each other and would kill each other at sight would yet, had I required shelter of any one of them, have guarded me, respected my person, and ceased warfare until my departure.

Shots were resounding somewhere near us, daytime though it was, and a shot in 'No Man's Land' is not an ordinary event. Once we were held up while two rival clan snipers tried their skill at each other across the road. Neither touched us; it was a private war. Eventually one fell off his rock, the other wished peace upon us—this struck me as being particularly appropriate—and waved his hand for us to pass.

It was an everyday affair with him and I expect one day some other sniper got him. The strange thing to me was that the women of these rival clans go about their usual duties, carrying water, driving cattle, and are never shot. No brigand, however infamous, would kill a woman. Women, these rough warriors say, are sacred. They wear scarlet trousers in order to be easily seen in the distance. These women, nevertheless, can shoot as straight as any clansman, and at a later date I had experience of their marksmanship. They can take to the loop-holed towers with unfaltering courage, and more than one man has missed the inheritance life would have brought but for the unerring aim of one of these warrior women.

These clansmen were always willing to give us water or sherbet—a sweet drink made of fruit juice—and could not do enough or offer us enough when they knew who we were. Their hospitality reminded me of home. Yet one would have excused inhospitality in a place where fruit was almost a luxury and often had to be brought many days' journey from India or Afghanistan.

Again we halted, for the *Asr* or afternoon prayer, just as we had performed the *Zuhr* previously.

From time to time we saw men ploughing the inhospitable land, trying to wrest a living from a country which seemed ever to resist their desires. All had rifles slung over their shoulders; around them were black-looking boulders, frowning down upon them as though in anger and perpetual defiance. In other stretches there were mulberry-trees clustering over the sides of the mountain.

Several times shots were fired in our direction as a challenge; a voice, sounding almost unearthly between the high rocks and the stillness, shouted, "Friend or foe?" and always we called back, "Friend! Peace be upon you." I listened eagerly and excitedly for the reply, "Peace be upon you too." Our escort then fired two blank shots, in case the voice assuring the clansman of our peaceful intentions did not reach him. At any rate there are occasions when it is as well to make assurance doubly sure. Sometimes when the occasion demanded it one of our guards would wave his *tulwar* in the air to denote that we belonged to the family of a chief, whereupon the raider up in the hills would fire three blank shots, giving us salutations and welcome through that part of the land and his assurances of good feeling towards us.

Thus we journeyed. Dusk began to fall just as we reached the friendly anchorage of another village khan, with whom we were to spend the night. The next afternoon would see us at our destination.

This khan was known as a deeply religious man. Our arrival coincided with the evening prayer, after which, washed of our travel stains, we were given a feast of pilau—a delicious dish of rice with aromatics—and roast chickens. The hill air makes appetites keen, and we enjoyed the meal heartily. It seemed quite an easy matter to eat four square meals a day. Mutton and rice appeared to be the staple diet, but there are so many ways of cooking the sheep that it never tastes twice the same.

After the meal the clansmen danced round the camp-fire with flashing *tulwars*. We women got the best view, looking down from the latticed windows. Suddenly in the midst of the dancing shots rang out. As though the wand of a fairy had transformed the scene, the men turned from dancers to soldiers. There was no 'scene.' The women drew back into their rooms, the men shouted orders to each other. A rival clansman was raiding the Khan's fort. Word was somehow sent to the enemy by lighted torches that guests were being entertained. More shots meaning retiral were heard, and the dancing was resumed. The women crept back to the lattice. To them, looking down again on the gleaming steel and whirling figures, the interlude might have been part of the dance.

That night my husband and I slept in a windowless heavily barred turret; the fort was guarded by thirty armed watchmen. I wondered, as I fell asleep exhausted after the excitements of the tiring day, whether yet I should wake up to find myself back in Scotland. Dawn, however, brought back the reality. We awoke to the "changing of the guard" with still a long exciting journey before us ere we reached our destination.

CHAPTER IV

IN THE WARRIOR CHIEFTAIN'S FORT

WE had breakfast and left the kindly shelter of the Khan's. The ten men forming the guard lent us by our previous host now returned home to their fort, and their place was taken by ten of a similar type belonging to our present host. These men would accompany us until we reached the safety of my husband's home, where if all went well we ought to arrive late that afternoon. The nearer we approached the more apprehensive I became.

The way became bare and desolate. It was indeed a wild land. It only required a terrible storm with thunder and lightning to turn it into a nightmare. Yet the heavily armed men who surrounded us were enough to absolve the most chicken-hearted from fear of personal violence in any case. I began to enter into the spirit of the land. It had appealed to me from the first. Here I would never require to look for adventure; it would find me. It lurked everywhere. The very stillness was mysterious, gripping. Some of the men sang songs, others recited couplets from poets, others remained silent, but all seemed in the best of spirits. If they were not looking for trouble, I thought, there was no reason for me to do so. I watched their faces from time to time, expecting them to turn their heads as we passed suspicious-looking rocks and crevices, or gaze up into the boulders, but they plodded steadily ahead.

Presently, after about two hours' journey, we saw two men approaching us on horseback. They held up their hands on nearing us, and our men drew up. What could this be? Between the arrival of the horsemen and the time of explanation there was nothing I had not imagined!

These men were sent by their khan—whose sentries had seen us passing on the road beneath his fort—to ask us to accept his hospitality and wait in his fort for a few hours until a conference then being held in his fort was over. He would explain on our arrival.

We were not very pleased to be diverted from our way, as this would make our arrival at the Chieftain's fort a late one, and it is no country to be out late at night in! However, there was nothing else to do but follow the two horsemen. A long tortuous path led to the Khan's fort. Arrived there we were met in the courtyard by that worthy himself, who greeted us loudly and warmly. He was an exceptionally tall man, and upright for his years. The scars of many fights seared his face; the light of battle was in his eye. He was a formidable enemy even to-day. As he talked to us he lightly fingered an armoury of weapons that clanked upon his body, much as one would in an idle moment swing a walking-stick. After the manner of the tribesmen when on adventure bent he wore his turban low, with one end over his mouth. His followers were dressed in the same way. To judge from their arms and their warlike appearance, it certainly seemed likely that—as report had it—they had held the pass for eighteen days against four times their number.

The old warrior advanced towards us, and explained that he had been appointed the head of four clans who were contemplating a raid into 'the foreigners'' country beyond Peshawar, and that he thought our lives would be greatly endangered at that time. Had we been 'foreigners' or British it would have been impossible for us to have escaped the wrath of any of the tribesmen who felt keenly the embargo maintained against them by the British at Peshawar; for a month ago some hill brigands, quite unknown to these clans, had made a raid for arms and ammunition on the troops, and since then the clansmen had been forbidden to pass into the city. Any other commodity they could go without except salt, and as this had all been used up during the past month they were desperate, and after much arguing had arrived at the conclusion that the only solution to the problem was a raid.

We remained there an hour and a half until all the pros and cons had been thoroughly discussed. When all had finished the oldest man there, who had been silent since our arrival, rose and said, "Give me but a moment of speech, O Khan! See, both my legs and arms have been broken, and my ribs too. Do you think at this age I boast of these things? Nay! This came about because I went hastily to fight. Look at these wound-marks to-day across my face! They are but to remind me how foolish is hot blood and the love of being first in the fray. Be patient, I beg of you all, bring not death too soon!"

But this advice from experience only brought jeers and loud laughs from the younger men. They threw pieces of stick at the man who had lived long enough to regret past battles—too long, to their way of thinking, and they did not hesitate to tell him so.

The Khan now spoke. His rising commanded silence. He surveyed the gathering. He was strength among the strong. "What is death? Why do you speak of wounds? Have not I for forty years been riddled with bullets and yet have not died? If you, at your age, are afraid to fight, O son of a jackal, it would be better for you to wear jewellery and scarlet trousers so that every one would think you a woman and would not harm you!"

It looked for a few moments as though the warriors might not have to go far for their fight, but things quietened down, and we set off on our journey once more.

The way became wilder yet, though here and there in the terrace-like uplands more cultivation appeared, and later on in the afternoon when we were yet some distance from our goal we saw on all the surrounding hill-tops great blazing bonfires. These my husband explained were a welcome to us by all the surrounding chiefs.

"You will see something round this next corner," said my husband. "Guess what it is?"

"Brigands!" I replied, fearing the worst.

"No, home."

"Home!" For a moment the very word itself sounded foreign to me. As we slowly made our way to that corner I thought of the peaceful home I knew, the quiet ordinary safe life I had led, my brother, the day I hooked the salmon——

The cavalcade had stopped. "What do you think of it? Wonderful, isn't it?" The words came to me hazily. My husband was beside me looking away up into the hills. "There is your new home, Morag."

My new home! I looked up and saw a grey loopholed wall neither welcoming nor inspiring, unless it were with awe. It was hung with bunting; a huge bonfire burned near it on another hill-top. My eyes grew misty as I looked at the distant welcome. These people were doing their utmost to make me happy. At that moment I knew the wholly unenviable feeling of being a 'foreigner.' The rest of the day seemed a dream. Up and up we climbed. What would my new relations be like, I wondered. Would they like me, and I them? Suppose they did not like me! My tortured thoughts came to an end. I had arrived at my new home.

As we, my husband and I, entered first the courtyard, a very tall dignified man approached us slowly, giving us time to dismount before he reached us. My husband helped me to alight and turning round I saw him kneel before the tall man and kiss his hands.

"My father," said Syed. I kissed his hands too, and he bent low to kiss my forehead. His dignity and height were so great that I suddenly felt small and speechless.

"Welcome, my son, and welcome to you, my daughter, to this your home! We are proud to-day to welcome you. You must now be tired after your long journey." He picked up our little daughter and turned towards the house. We followed. Syed squeezed my hand reassuringly as my knees knocked together, and, amid a volley of shots from the clansmen gathered to greet us, we passed along the beautiful carpets laid down in our honour into our new home. The fort itself was a huge black building with high grey loopholed towers at each corner, obviously built to resist attack. To-day it was hung with bunting which softened its usually military-looking coldness.

Servants stood all along the corridors as we passed to the harem or women's part of the house. I would have liked to wash myself and put on other garments before meeting my new relations, but my husband said they would naturally be very eager to see us and would not keep us long.

My mother-in-law and her daughters were awaiting us expectantly, and came forward at once as we entered the room. The old Chief presented me, and his wife at once embraced me warmly, kissing me on both cheeks. She was a tall, remarkably young-looking woman, with lovely dark flashing eyes and the fair skin of the women of that part. Ceremoniously she bade me welcome, and was so courteous and charming that I liked her immediately. Her daughters now came forward with Margaret clinging to their hands. They resembled their mother both in looks and manner, and their long three-quarter tunics, gauzy head-veils, and gold-embroidered slippers made them look like fairy-tale princesses. This welcome over, they led me to my rooms on the first floor and insisted upon helping me in every way possible.

The low-ceilinged room was long, with white-washed walls. A thick plush curtain hung over the main entrance. The long, narrow window was placed high in the wall; rugs covered the floor and a large low bed like a divan occupied one corner, with a low brass-topped Indian table by its side. On a shelf over the bed lay a copy of the holy Koran covered with a silk cloth, for the Koran must never be placed under any other books or on the floor. Another curtain hid a number of shelves where clothes might be kept.

At the far corner of the room a second door opened into a large bathroom. Stone steps led down to the bath, the top of which was level with the floor. No water was laid on, but there was a filled tin bath, and several tin water-jugs ranged along-side were evidently used for carrying hot water when required. I was wondering how many cans of water would be necessary to fill the stone bath when a maid bearing a deep copper bowl of hot water entered from the bedroom. This she placed on a low wooden table.

She took me completely in charge in a masterful manner and washed me as a grown-up washes a child. The colour of the water made me wonder what my new relations must have thought when they first saw me.

My trunks were being carried in by the men-servants while my face-washer, joined by another maid, gave instructions as to where the luggage was to be placed. There appeared to be a slight altercation regarding a box which had been badly knocked about before we reached the Khyber. One of the maids seemingly thought a rather fierce-looking servant had been responsible for the damage, and in spite of his denials she slapped his face.

The face-washer and face-slapper turned out to be a thoroughly capable person in every way, and soon unlocked my trunks. Before my arrival I had imagined servants who would probably watch me round the edge of a door, and leave me to do all the unpacking for myself. But here were two women who had never before seen a Western woman, yet now, without displaying any obvious interest in me, were unpacking my clothes as though they had never done anything else in their lives. It gave me the feeling of being insignificant and unimportant. The coats, skirts, and frocks they were putting away suddenly seemed drab, uninteresting, and unromantic. I remembered having worn an Eastern dress once at a party at home, when it appeared too colourful and even bizarre. Here for some reason it seemed the only suitable dress.

Overcome by curiosity I opened another door and saw menservants putting Syed's luggage into a room similar to my own. My first fears were stilled. After all, there seemed to be no harem as I had imagined it. We were to be allowed rooms to ourselves and would not be obliged to crowd in with the rest of the family, as well-meaning friends assured me would be the case; moreover, we each had a separate bathroom.

Tribesmen in the Courtyard of a Frontier Chieftain's Fort

My sisters-in-law interrupted further comparisons by asking from the door whether they might come in. Their arms were full of garments of every colour of the rainbow, specially made for me by them on the strength of measurements Syed thought would be suitable! Eagerly they watched me transform myself into a chieftain's daughter. When I had put on the heelless gold-embroidered slippers they laughed at my faltering steps in the unaccustomed shoes. Then they amused themselves by putting on my coats and skirts. They both kissed me affectionately and were so unaffected and vivacious that I liked them immediately; we might have known each other for years. The misery I had gone through at the thought of meeting these relations of my husband seemed to have been the misapplication of much hard and distressing thinking. Yet here we were, in spite of the language bar between us, perfectly happy and at ease in each other's company.

The blue satin trousers were certainly comfortable; peg-topped and cleverly draped, they looked like a skirt. The three-quarter tunic and gauzy veil added a touch of mystery. By the time I had negotiated a few rounds of the room even the slippers had lost all terrors, and I felt one of the family.

The girls clapped their hands and laughed at my anxiety as to my appearance. Each took one of my hands and we passed along the balcony to where shouts and a great splashing of water proclaimed that Margaret was not experiencing any difficulty with either language or environment.

From the windows there appeared nothing but stretches of wild hills. They thrilled me, and I promised myself future exploration; when I later found that this was strictly forbidden, it of course seemed all the more desirable.

Down below, the courtyard looked like a fair. Hundreds of stalwart clansmen who had trekked from the Kohistan (Highlands) were arriving in a stream. Thirsty and tired like ourselves they must have been, but they were not going to let that mar the occasion. Every now and again a volley of welcome rang through the courtyard. Some came on ponies, some on dromedaries, some on donkeys, but all were well and truly armed. How, I wondered, in my Western way, were all these people going to be accommodated?

Selima and Halima, my sisters-in-law, told me they were having the feast of welcome that night. "But not for all those people?" I asked. "No, there are yet more to come," they replied, "and there are many tents and *shamianas* put up for them."

They pointed through the latticed balcony wall to where the tents were still going up in the gardens. It looked already like a vast city of canvas, dwarfed by the towering hills. What a welcome to give a foreigner, I thought! The hospitality of the hills is the same everywhere. My heart warmed to these people, many of whom, judging by their travel-worn appearance, had come long distances to greet me. The past for me now was dead. I was Morag Abdullah now, and must live up to the name.

CHAPTER V

MY BEAUTIFICATION AS A BRIDE

SYED'S mother and sisters were tremendously excited about our wedding, which was to take place at once. For the old Chieftain did not think we were properly married until he had seen the ceremony in his own hills and with his own eyes! Personally, having already been through two marriage ceremonies I was quite content—but what girl can resist being the centre of attraction?

In the absence of my mother it was arranged for my mother-in-law's sister to be my foster-mother for the occasion. The next day I was escorted in great style to her house a few miles away. She received me with supreme ceremony and led me through rooms festooned with roses in my honour. Once in my room she closed the door and told me excitedly about the preparations for the wedding. It was to be a huge affair. Every clansman able to walk, ride, or be carried was to be there; all their wives, daughters, and servants would accompany them.

I told her I had already seen the guests' tents in my father-in-law's fort gardens. "That would be only a few of them," she replied. "There is still a week before the ceremony, and many more will yet arrive."

One could scarcely have expected such a crowd even in the middle of a great city, but then there are clannish people outside Scotland! Between the relations whose duty it was to be there, the lesser chieftains whose privilege it was to present themselves, and those who had simply wanted to share the enjoyment, surely every clan, hostile and friendly, must have mustered!

My foster-mother was a stout, jolly woman, the mother of five tall sons, to whom she was devoted. She had thought of everything for my comfort; sympathized with me because I was so far away from home, and assured me I would find in her the kindness and love of all my missing relatives! She talked by the hour of my husband, and I found she had had no small share in soothing the feelings of my father-in-law when the cable came asking for his consent to our marriage.

Next day my beautification treatment started with a bath of asses' milk. I laughed while preparing for it, and wondered whether this was a superstition or whether it really had any beautifying value. After remaining in it for nearly half an hour there was no question as to its beneficial effect. My skin was softened and felt fresh. I wondered how it was possible for the milk bath to be so warm and was told there were special cauldrons heated over a fire which were used only on these occasions.

Next morning I was given a fragrant rose-water bath. Then a rare henna-coloured oil, scented with sandalwood, was rubbed into my hair by a maid with capable hands; after three applications I was shampooed with what looked like a piece of leather and proved to be a kind of soap which kept hair from becoming dry. The treatment made my hair marvellously glossy and as though it had been freshly waved. Now another maid applied refreshing sweet-scented creams to my face, neck, arms and hands, while an elderly woman massaged my legs and arms. My nails were hennaed.

A peculiar roller-shaped stone was then gently rubbed all over my body. It had an almost electrical effect. I felt refreshed and able to do anything. This special treatment would make one a fortune in a few months in the West. Unfortunately it is a guarded secret. The strange thing about this stone is that, although it is hard like flint to the touch, when applied with a rotary movement to the skin it feels soft as velvet and quite warm.

The final treatment was a bath in a heavily scented milky substance. I was not dried, but placed on a bed where I lay until the stuff became hard like one of the Western beauty packs. It took about an hour, and little glowing charcoal braziers were placed about the room to keep me from feeling cold. The quiet of it all and the newness of the treatment took all my previous tiredness away. I might have been resting for years, though only a few days ago I had arrived exhausted after the long journey.

When the 'pack' dried it was softened with rose-water—of which there seemed no shortage—and gently removed. After this followed an hour's massage, during which I fell asleep, and I had to be awakened when it was finished.

At the end of the treatment when I was dressed, my foster-mother came to ask how I had liked it, and was delighted when told I felt new!

"Early to rest to-night for the wedding and the feast to-morrow," she said.

We walked out on the little balcony and looked at the clansmen. The canvas village seemed to have transferred itself from our fort here. Laughter, song, and bustle filled the air. As each new guest arrived a volley rang out from his party. I began to wonder how I could ever go through with the next day, and said so to my hostess.

"We are trying to make you feel at home now you are one of us." The reply touched me and as I looked through the latticed wall at the huge crowd of my new countrymen I felt grateful to them for their loyalty to me, a foreigner, in a land where a foreigner is particularly unwelcome.

All this time I did not see my husband. Every day he sent messages to me like the letters he used to write to me in the old Edinburgh days.

That night when all had gone to bed early in anticipation of the morrow's celebration, I looked from my window across the hills. Their grey heights made me feel homesick. I wondered whether the moon shining there so coldly bright looked down on the hills of home. Had I made a mistake to leave them? And out there on the balcony, seeing the tents of the sleeping guests, I felt it disloyal to them to harbour any doubts. The warmth of their greeting was answer enough to my question.

I was too excited to sleep much that night and by

early morning had just dozed off when my door was opened and my sisters-in-law and my hostess entered, carrying ropes of roses which they festooned round my bed. Servants came next bearing armfuls of many-coloured materials, others carried golden slippers, others had mysterious-looking boxes. All wished me happy greetings, speaking slowly that the words might be understood.

Another rose-water bath, breakfast, and then the dressing for the ceremony started. From the courtyard came loud calls. My foster-mother walked out veiled on to the balcony to receive the good wishes of the guests for the bride. She returned thanks for me and gave the guests welcome on my behalf and her own.

Games were arranged. The young men vied with each other as to who would carry off the honours. Others rode unbroken horses with tact and style—it required both!

The girls and women watched all these games with the keenest interest from behind their latticed walls, and although the men must have known, if only from the continuous chattering, that we were there, they gave no sign that they were aware of our presence.

It looked a gay and jolly gathering and one could in these circumstances only remotely associate warfare with these men. To-day they had forgotten it. No rival chieftain worthy of the name would raid his enemy when there were wedding celebrations. It was a strange sight. The men were of all ages, dressed in their gayest holiday clothes, their big turbans adding to their height—and many must have been nearly seven feet tall. The sun glinted on the gold embroidery of their waistcoats and glanced off their swords as they danced round to a war chant. I noticed the curious fact that so many people made very little noise. The hills seemed to absorb the sounds of the chatter and sword clashing, shooting and horse-racing. Prizes were given, and to judge by the applause the winners each had a considerable following. There was the greatest acclamation, which rose wave upon wave, when an old man with a long white beard received first prize for a sword dance. "Had I been thirty years younger," he called, "I would have challenged you all to any game or sport you cared to mention." The applause broke out again louder than ever.

My proxy mother now came for me to dress. My bedroom was a bower of scented flowers. My face was so fresh and rosy from the last week's treatments that my 'dresser' decided I needed no cosmetics. My mother-in-law gave me my wedding outfit as one of her presents. The long veil was pink ninon of cobweb fineness, sewn with scintillating stones and edged with gold lace. The three-quarter jumper, long-sleeved, was of finest rose-pink velvet, and the baggy trousers, tight round the ankles, of gold cloth. This cloth is spun from real gold and no garment made of it ever wears out or loses its sheen. All the clothes were hand-made by my sisters-in-law and their maids, and looked lovely enough in colour and texture to have belonged to a hill sprite.

Excitedly I dressed—putting on the gold-embroidered slippers last. As I stood before the glass the onlookers clapped their hands in ecstasy. Never, they said, had they seen so lovely a bride, not even those years ago when the five beautiful sisters were married on five consecutive days! I was delighted that they were satisfied and hugged them for sheer delight.

As we walked to the reception room where I was to meet other chieftains' wives and daughters, servants were carrying in great loads.

"Your presents," gleefully murmured my sister-in-law Selima. "There are caravans and caravans of them. Carpets, shawls, rugs, jewellery, clothes, fur coats, fruits, nuts, and hundreds of other things." In my excitement I had not thought of the possibility of presents. I felt giddy with expectation. I could not help contrasting our two simple weddings in a war-ruined country with this grand affair away 'at the back of beyond.'

My elder sister-in-law came to say that a chieftain relative had brought two lovely horses for me with silver-embossed saddles. But by now I was too overwhelmed to understand fully what anybody said to me. Arrived at the reception hall, I was presented to the other hill-chieftains' wives and daughters. Their lovely clothes, of every colour of the rainbow, made me gasp with delight. I stood for a few seconds thinking the scene might disappear, so unreal did it all seem.

The elder wives and daughters of our neighbours kissed my forehead, the younger ones my hands.

They behaved with charm and dignity, and without any whispering among themselves as to their first opinion of the newcomer, which I had dreaded. I might have been their queen whom they had seen every day of her life in precisely the same manner. I learned that day a lesson in perfect manners. Here were women none of whom had ever crossed into a foreign land, many of whom had never even been away from their own hills, amazing me with their deportment and politeness!

I was asked to sit down. The oldest chieftain's wife came and handed me a large silver casket. "These," she explained, "were bought in far-away Hindustan."

"For you," my sister-in-law said.

I opened it and found a long string of magnificent pearls, with bracelets, earrings, head-ornaments, and rings to match. The beauty and costliness of the gift took my breath away. I thanked her as graciously as my beating heart would allow. Then came a procession of similar presents. Each set was in its own box and the box from my mother-in-law was of gold studded with rubies, diamonds, and emeralds! After I had examined each my servants carried it to a guarded room.

So totally different was this scene from the one I had just witnessed in the men's courtyard that the sense of unreality was intensified. The more gifts I received, the more like a fairy-tale it became. I remember wondering just how these people had carried such treasures safely through that brigand country. Tears of gratitude mingled with the gems.

It was the most wonderful time I had ever had in my life.

A servant came to ask whether the bride was ready for the ceremony. Truth to tell, the bride would gladly have gone to her own room and relieved her feelings with a good cry.

CHAPTER VI

MY MARRIAGE CEREMONY

MY proxy mother arranged my clothes, fastened my *yashmak*, and taking my hand led me to the doorway—the others followed quietly behind. All along the passages and in every room as we passed I saw crowds of women; everywhere there were scented roses. Slowly we made our way to the farther end of the house. We entered a lofty room and stood on a small platform near a curtain which divided the room into two, while the other women guests moved into their places on the same side. Peeping round a corner of the curtain I saw the men coming in. My husband, whom I had not seen for a week, stood on the other side of the curtain just beside where I was. My proxy mother laid a restraining hand on my arm when I forgot myself and was about to raise the curtain to speak to Syed. More shuffling—then silence.

"The *mullah!*" whispered my proxy mother. Round the corner of the curtain I watched the priest approach—an old man with an immensely long white beard, robed in black, with the demeanour of a general. He saluted from time to time as he came along and then stepped up to the platform where my husband was. The silence was unbroken until the *mullah* led the prayer. Then he faced the curtain and asked three times:

"Morag Murray, daughter of an illustrious clan, do you accept Syed Abdullah, son of a great chief, as your husband with a dowry of a thousand pounds?"

I replied "Yes" each time. When the question was put to my husband I hoped he would not have any cause to change his mind. He had not! Another prayer; then the *mullah* said:

"Clansmen, we have this day witnessed the sight of our Chief's son married to the daughter of an illustrious and courageous clan from a far country beyond the seas. May it be the will of Allah to grant them happiness, keep them faithful to one another, and give them His blessing!"

My proxy mother pulled back the curtain, I took my husband's hand and stood beside him, veiled, before all the clansmen. They bowed as one man deeply and graciously, and placing their hands on their swords gave their promise to protect and aid both the Chief's son and the wife of the Chief's son. I bowed to all corners of the room and retired gladly behind the curtain. The men went out first to the courtyard, where more volleys were fired, and then there was a perfect thunder of good wishes. There was no mistaking the warmth of the wishes, nor of the sincerity; these were plain people who could not hide their feelings. I felt glad they had received me so generously in the 'Free Land,' for the past was past. I was now one of the clanswomen.

A rest now, a few cups of delicious straw-coloured green tea. Excited talks about the lovely gifts which I had had no time to examine—a change of dress into a deep yellow ninon veil sequin-sewn, a deep yellow velvet jumper, and shimmering green and gold cloth trousers. This was the feast night. Every available cook in the district had been lent, and as every chieftain brought his own servants the problem of overwork did not exist.

A cloth was spread on the carpet, and we sat down cross-legged in the rose-decked room. It was amazing how so many people could be accommodated even in relays, though the rooms were large and connected with one another like a series of dining-rooms. Dishes piled up with delicious rice hid tender chickens. Little fat discs of roasted meat eaten with home-made bread; whole sheep disappearing almost magically; roast mutton steeped in butter delicately flavoured; saffron-coloured rice, with each grain soft and yet separated from the rest, strewn with pistachio nuts and small round sultanas; a delicious white pudding like whipped cream covered with what looked like smooth silver paper, which dissolved instantaneously as one ate it; tasty 'candies' and large juicy melons, dried mulberries and walnuts—these are a few scattered recollections of that wonderful meal. The servants waited upon us with tireless energy. As soon as one's plate was empty (and often before) another helping appeared as by magic. Having had little to eat all day, I was able to do justice to the feast—so I hoped, indeed, for I did not want to spoil the feast by stopping too soon, as I knew the women were afraid I should think the food was not good enough. It was a great relief to me when I saw signs of satisfaction on surrounding faces.

From the hills again we saw the bonfires celebrating the marriage. For a long time that night Syed and I stood watching the great flames leap higher and higher jagging into the blackness while we talked over the happenings of the previous week. Round us there was silence, for the guests having thoroughly overeaten had gone to sleep. The bonfires alone seemed alive, challenging the foreigner in their midst to prove herself worthy of her new clan, or to question whether anything was wanting in the welcome.

The next day we returned to our fort, and days more were spent admiring the gifts. No names were attached to any of the innumerable carpets, rugs, shawls, saddles, slippers, gold cloth, which composed the array, and I felt at a loss how to thank the anonymous givers until my mother-in-law told me no thanks were expected. The donors considered themselves sufficiently thanked by my acceptance. I gloated over the beauty of the gifts. Where, I wondered, in those bare hills did all these lovely things come from? Some had no doubt been levied as taxes from merchants whose caravans passed through the clansmen's territory and paid for safe conduct. Carpets came from Bokhara on camel-back. The jewellery had been made in India and the fruits came from the clansmen's well-stocked orchards.

From time to time I came upon small parcels containing strange indefinable objects. My sisters-in-law laughed and explained to me that these were luck-bringers, though Muslims are by religion forbidden to believe in 'luck.' Highland folks, however, all over the world seem specially interested in omens good and bad. One specially bulky package, more carefully done up than any of the beautiful jewellery, contained a piece of the skin of a pure white lamb! This had been dried and was accounted a great rarity. If I kept this always carefully, the giver had written, its presence would ensure my safety in any part of the hills. Another object enclosed in much bleached linen proved to be the tooth of a saint! This, if kept always within reach, would bring the answer to any prayer. My Highland nature forced me to think something of these amulets, although I could not help being amused at the almost childish way in which they had been wrapped up.

After the presents had been thoroughly examined a conference was held. Both my parents-in-law were convinced that we would feel much freer and happier in a home of our own. They came to the arrangement that we might occupy one of the Chieftain's forts some miles distant.

The fact that I had not seen a newspaper or heard any outside news dawned on me after ten days! Anyhow I should have had no time to read newspapers, and the place seemed so bound up in itself that for us the world beyond the hills did not exist. A magnificent-looking postman on horseback, well armed, carried the mail, but the ordinary news went by the travellers and merchants. In this way a story from the hills being retold in Peshawar lost nothing in the repeated tellings, for the clansmen are finished artists where story-telling is concerned, and no good story is short.

The wedding guests melted away back to their homes among the distant hills, while we were now busily engaged arranging for our departure to the new fort. Servants were sent on ahead to prepare the place, but as it was simply furnished like my father-in-law's, we had only our personal belongings and gifts to transport. The presents were a 'flitting' in themselves, several caravans being required to take them. Syed's relatives accompanied us when we started a week later. Poor villagers who had heard of the arrival gathered to share in any charity that might be dispensed at such an auspicious time. They were given as much fruit and nuts as they could carry and amid their blessings we passed into the fort.

Splendid hills reared themselves on every side, frowning, rocky, mysterious. One particularly, shaped like a cone, attracted my attention and admiration. "How lovely!" I exclaimed. My younger sister-in-law who was beside me looked meaningly at me as though intimating silence. I said no more until we were alone in the room, when she told me:

"That hill is of great importance to us and the other clans round here. When any of the clans are about to raid another they watch that hill carefully. It is called 'the hill of the White Lady' because sometimes a woman in white with flowing scarf walks slowly up its slope. At the very top, which is pointed and dangerous to stand upon, she waves her scarf. That is a signal that no raid must take place, or famine will be throughout the land. The clansmen think more of the White Lady's warning than of any of the old men's wisdom. Unfortunately the White Lady does not always appear, but whenever a raid is threatened we pray to Allah to avert it, while in our hearts we long for the White Lady to walk."

"Do you believe in the White Lady?" I asked.

"We all believe in her. It was said once that long ago the clansmen took no notice of her warning and on that occasion many clans were almost destroyed and never had there been such a year of desolation and raiding. The story has so frightened the clansmen that no matter what raid is afoot the White Lady by appearing can stop it."

"I should like to see this White Lady. It may be but a masquerading coward who fears to lose his life," I said.

"Speak not so, my sister! I greatly fear the wrath of the White Lady, and as there is a very powerful enemy of my father's just over the hill, we must not say such things. Our men do not fear death, but the calamity of their crops being spoiled and their cattle and sheep dying mysteriously, as may happen if the warning is disregarded."

My sister-in-law was now thoroughly nervous. Putting her hand into the neck of her jumper she drew out a tiny silver box, and, looking round anxiously lest she might be overheard, said in a low, frightened voice, "This talisman ensures that the clansmen should always pay dutiful respect to the

White Lady. I shall give it to you, my sister, and I pray to Allah you may be privileged to see the mysterious one."

It was a pretty legend, I thought, and, being accustomed to stories of kelpies, brownies, wee-folk, and warlocks, I soon forgot it.

We settled down in our new home, delighted to be alone with our little daughter again, and the days were spent arranging everything to our liking. Living in a fort guarded by tall armed sentries and dressed in my Eastern clothes, I felt like a medieval lady, held at ransom yet thoroughly enjoying the experience.

Each morning our cook presented himself for the day's orders. He cut quite a romantic figure in spotless white peg-topped trousers, turban, and shirt. He carried an alarming-looking knife, thrust in a businesslike way in his *kummerbund*; whether this was for effect, for the purpose of dealing with certain foods requiring cutting up, or in the hope of being prepared for the revenge he might have harboured in his heart against some old foe, I cannot say. The weapon in any case did not hamper his memory, and I never knew him to forget the smallest item in the daily menu.

Sometimes our fare consisted of roasted mutton studded with cloves, eaten with pistachio-flavoured rice and thin fried bread, made of fine oaten flour, and served hot and deliciously crisp. Or we might have roast chickens piled over with saffron rice and served with small meat-balls mint-flavoured. The puddings were rich, and many contained such ingredients as almonds, whole and ground, walnuts treated in mysterious ways, or apples and oranges in in thick syrup. Appetites are appetites in 'No Man's Land,' and do not require any encouragement. Yet, in spite of the amount of food eaten, indigestion is unknown, nor have sugar or sweets any detrimental effect on the teeth of the clansmen. The nearest dentist was in Peshawar, and I never spoke to anyone who had required his services up in the hills.

To return to the business of the kitchen. While the orders were being given to the cook, the maid-servant whose duty it was brought the weighing-machine on to the balcony, while an attendant carried sacks containing flour, sugar, a large basket with vegetables, and everything necessary for the day's meals. Sitting cross-legged the maid weighed out the quantities required. The store sacks and fruit or vegetables not needed were locked up again and the huge door-key was once again suspended from the maid's waist-belt. We were not veiled before the menservants, as all were old retainers whose grandfathers had been employed by the clan.

In the village were shops filled with fruit, nuts, skins, fur caps, etc. The grocer is a general merchant, and replenishes his stock when caravans return from across the Frontier. The caravans travelling to India take quantities of sheep-skin coats, fruit and nuts, fat-tailed sheep and hill-bred ponies. Sometimes exchanges are made, or the goods are sold for hard cash. It is at these times that jewellery is purchased, or anything the clanswomen require. There is always great excitement before a caravan leaves, as anything forgotten must wait until the next caravan goes.

The general idea of the average person in the West regarding the Pathan country is that of a stretch of inhospitable hills bristling with snipers, whose sole aim is to shoot a white man. There is indeed much clan warfare, yet to say the entire area is infested with brigands and that pot-shooting is their pastime is an injustice to the gallant men of a great race. True it is, too, that if a clansman shows cowardice he must become an outlaw unless he treks to Afghanistan or India, where he can always obtain employment. Should he become a brigand in his own hills, and live by his wits, he is as much an enemy of the clansmen as of any other traveller through that part.

The lack of water is the outstanding difficulty, because agriculture for the most part supplies the people with a living. Practically all blood-feuds there trace their origin to some such incident as a dispute about the right of a certain man to water his fields from a certain place. When once a life has been taken by one of the clansmen, it is the turn of the murdered man's clan to seek revenge. On it goes, an eye for an eye, from generation to generation. The inhospitable soil, which is practically seventy-five per cent. shale and small stones, allows but scanty cultivation on the terraced hills and where Nature is so unkind a mother ordinary laws cannot apply to her children.

The territory, nearly eight hundred miles long,

lies between Chinese Turkestan in the north and Baluchistan in the south, and separates India from Afghanistan. It contains about seventy-eight clans whose characteristics, manner of living, loves and hates, and moral codes are very similar, so that my own experiences in one section of the country may legitimately be regarded as representative of the whole.

Generally speaking, a clan of several thousand souls inhabits a district divided into a number of villages of which the one where the Chieftain lives is the capital. Each village is completely encircled by a high wall some seven feet thick made of dried clay mixed with chopped hay, which is as hard as stone. Four gateways, which are securely bolted at sunset, are each surmounted by a windowed turret so constructed that the six stalwart clansmen who keep watch through the night can let themselves down on either the inside or the outside of the wall in case of emergency. The Chief's house is built of stone, rough-hewn on the outside, but inside the walls are plastered and often papered. The village houses are of either sun-dried clay bricks or stone; some are double-storied, others even three-storied.

The fort, or Chief's house, is usually on an artificial eminence in the middle of the village. It too is surrounded by high walls with watch-towers and gateways which are closed at dusk. Inside the wall there is a great courtyard, about three or four acres in extent, round which are the rooms of men-servants and retainers who have no families. At the far end there is a sort of daïs—the Chief's durbar-hall, so to speak. Over this are his offices; and at the side a double-fronted gateway leads to the harem, or women's apartments.

Only women can pass through the gateway leading to the harem *serai*. As one enters, one comes upon a larger courtyard of five or six acres; in the middle there is a garden with sycamore trees along the pathway, leading to a fountain. At the far end of the fort there are ten or eleven rooms for the Chief's wife and daughters, daughter-in-law, and even the mother-in-law, who is as conspicuous as she is in the West. His sons and their wives are given rooms in the same courtyard, perhaps at the other side. The kitchens and store-rooms are apart from the living-rooms. As the servants of each family have to be accommodated there are often a hundred women in a chief's household, and one can forgive the stories, to which distance lends enchantment, that these poor harassed men have quite often fifty wives or "a harem full of women."

It is sorrowfully true that the chieftain is as henpecked as any Western man. Moreover, any woman widowed in clan warfare and unable to support herself is henceforth under the protection of the chief. This in itself is a fair proposition to tackle.

Surely the popular conception of an Eastern harem is the most elastic imaginable, perhaps because it is one of the very few things left about which there is yet mystery—or is it simply ignorance? My own ideas regarding harems, even modified by quite simple explanations of my husband's—which ought to have been sufficient exposition of the riddle

—stretched somewhat fearfully into the realms of naked bead-draped dancers with film-star allure, so that for days, which stretched into weeks after my arrival at my father-in-law's fort, I expected that some hitherto closed door would open and admit me into the Utopian harem which is believed to fill the dreams, if not the waking life, of Eastern men.

I was prepared, as one so often is, for everything but what actually happened. I could not associate my new relations with a harem; and yet the very word itself means 'sacred.' Surely, I reasoned, these discreetly dressed women could not possibly live in the harem. Inborn ideas, especially romantic ones, are so difficult to uproot, even when we are faced with sufficient first-hand knowledge to control our imagination.

The first visit I paid to a neighbouring fort offered the chance of the fulfilment of my yet unrealized hopes. Here I was confident of finding what harems are popularly supposed to contain. My excitement rose to effervescence as I was wafted along darkish corridors to the harem. A door swung open, and the room seemed packed with women and girls, whose ages probably ranged from sixteen to sixty; pretty, too, especially the younger women, considerably painted and altogether delightfully coy and promising. The Chief entered the room, and introduced to me, with a sweep of his hand which included the entire group of women, "my ladies." Wait, thought I, in the tiny lull that followed, until I see Syed! But the business—nay, the ordeal—of the 'Free Land' introduction is not disposed of by a sweep of the hand. Each woman melted into her place, and stood until the Chief presented her to me. This consisted of the preliminary giving of her name; a pause followed, then a recitation of all the attributes of the lady, followed by an account of the bravery of her clan, until I had visions of reaching the end of the line some time the following week.

By the time the last introduction was performed, I had been presented to the Chief's wife (sole and solitary), his wife's sisters and their daughters, his own sisters and their daughters, and a sprinkling of cousins who were spending that day at the fort. My disillusionment was complete. I wish I could entertain my readers with harem orgies of the 'Free Land'; be sure it would be done if there were material for it!

Polygamy is allowed by Islam, yet few men seem to avail themselves of the doubtful distinction of becoming lord and master of four wives. As one chief told me, "it was a costly and uncomfortable predicament," as according to Koranic injunctions each wife must be treated with the same amount of affection and be given equally comfortable apartments to herself; as another mighty warrior in the Pathan country told me, it was too much to expect even of himself! It was only after my return to the West that a film story renewed the old harem illusion. My sisters-in-law greatly enjoyed my confidences about what I had expected, and told me they believed every man in India had four wives!

CHAPTER VII

AT THE WHITE LADY'S HILL

AFTER the removal to our fort there was much to do putting the place in order. The wedding presents took weeks to arrange. I found occupation for the thirty servants quite easily, employing some making clothes or embroidering slippers and waist-coats for the men, while others carried messages to relations, constantly travelling between different forts. They also got the latest news and were more or less human newspapers.

I was secretly very anxious to experience a raid and hinted so to my husband—who said "God forbid!" so fervently that I wished it all the more! I began to think these men carried rifles and knives only as a pose, since for six months we had lived as peacefully as though we had been back in Edinburgh—perhaps more so, for there are no taxes, no civilized ways of being run over, no trains, no gas or electric-light bills to meet, no people collecting money for charity. I began to feel slightly disappointed with so much preparation for warfare that never seemed to happen. Besides, we lived high up on a rocky hill and it did not seem likely that armed guards and sentries would allow anyone on warfare bent to approach.

One day my younger sister-in-law came on horseback to visit us. "Bobo Jan,"[1] I said, "what happens when there is a raid?"

"Dear sister, speak not of it. Everything happens that God intended not to. Do not let us talk of it lest we bring one. I have seen two raids. Once it was when staying with a relative who was killed, with his two sons. His wife then defended the fort and commanded the men, and eventually aid arrived just in time to save the fort. I had never known fear until that day. How I prayed!"

The girl seemed to be living it over again as she grasped my arm and shuddered.

We walked in the garden almost until she went, and I began to think of exploring some of those harmless-looking hills, and particularly the hill of the White Lady. From time to time I watched caravans, like small beetles, crawling along the roads far below. Sometimes we heard cries of challenge carried far up to us on the clear air, for the absence of smoke makes a shout or shot ring almost like a bell. I knew it was no use asking my husband to allow me to explore, so started to lay my own plans by making myself the possessor of a woman-servant's clothes. It was somewhat of a shock to be told the hill was eight miles away. The difficulty would be to absent myself for sufficient time to get there, explore the place, and return home. I dared not take anybody into my confidence because if I were too long away the servants would be asked, and might, under pressure, own up. I had to play a lone hand. There was no road direct

[1] A term of endearment, as is also "Bhabi Jan."

to the hill, I found out from guarded questions, nor was there ever likely to be, in view of the superstition. My own opinion of the White Lady was that some holy man—not quite so holy as he might be—had taken refuge in a cave there, and with the help of a servant who carried food to him worked the 'stunt' himself. The servant, while visiting the surrounding forts as a poor man in need, would hear about a raid which might take place, and would report the news to his master, who, as these holy men are greatly afraid of personal violence, would know when to work the 'magic.'

These so-called holy men came from time to time to the fort. They spoke little, received food while they rested, and went their way. They called themselves saints. No doubt a good many of them were, but on the other hand a number were brigands' 'spies' taking stock of the land and especially the defences. To make assurance doubly sure, they were never allowed inside the inner wall of the fort. They slept, if they wanted to rest, in an outhouse, always guarded. Some of them had such long hair and beards and bushy eyebrows that there was scarcely any face to be seen. There was nobody to say they *were* saints, while it was equally impossible to say they were not brigands' spies. They travelled as saints and unarmed, dispensing blessings on all they passed. No traveller or brigand molested them, but even gave them help, food, or money, and it struck me that this might not be a bad profession!

Luck came my way one day. My husband was to accompany his father to visit a chief some ten or

A Khyber Tribesman in the Attitude of Sniping

A Holy Man of the Frontier

twelve miles away. I tried not to appear unduly relieved at the prospect of their absence and did not have much chance in any case as the fort guards were to be doubled for the time. It was going to be difficult to get out of the fort before I even considered the eight odd miles to the hill. Eventually the caravan was ready. My husband was very ill at ease at leaving me. "Promise me," he begged, "you will not go out of that gate." I promised, glad that he said nothing about going over the walls!

"Remember," he called back, "send a man at once on the fastest horse if you want me."

"All right," I called in reply, and the caravan set out.

They would be away at least one night, I thought, so that I must go that day to explore the hill; yet even after surmounting the difficulty of leaving I had to be careful to make myself as inconspicuous as possible.

First I sent messages to my mother-in-law to say I would not come to her that day as I would take the opportunity of writing to my relations in Britain. I had not intended visiting her, but was most anxious to make sure she would not visit me.

The best time for my departure I thought would be at the guards' meal-time, when there would be only a few men on the watch. The next meal being the evening one, I would have seven hours during which I might with comparative safety efface myself. At 11.30 A.M. I had my midday meal so that the servants saw me dressed as usual. Then I told my maids not to disturb me before the evening meal and that I expected a woman from another fort who knew the way to my apartments and need not be announced. There must have been many loopholes in my ruse, for after all I was a stranger and knew nothing of the ways of people outside the fort.

Once in my room, I shot the bolt across the door and dressed in the maidservant's clothes. Unfortunately she was short and I was tall, she was fat and I was thin, but the *burka* hid much that required hiding, and, as it is said that one touch of Nature makes the whole world kin, so one *burka* makes all women duplicates of each other! The disguise with the common leather shoes was so complete that I could hardly recognize myself.

It was now after twelve, and I hoped most of the men would be off duty. Unbarring the door I slipped out along the passage on my way to the back of the fort. The sentry on duty at the entrance to the house I had unfortunately forgotten. "Where are you going, handmaiden?" he challenged. "Peace be upon you," I replied in a squeaky voice; "I go on the private affairs of the wife of the Chief's son."

"Peace be upon you," came the reply. "Pass upon your way." Thus encouraged, I proceeded. This was going to be easy!

The next sentry was round the corner. I eyed him tremulously through the gauze 'eye-windows.'

"Why do you come here, senseless one? Have you perchance been gazing on the garden of roses and lost your way?"

"No," I replied, "I have stayed here too long

and my mistress requires the medicine I carry and will be greatly troubled by my absence."

"Why do you not get a horseman to carry it back, while you make your way with more safety?"

"The horseman might fall and break the bottle or might waste too much time talking to passing maids and be even later than I, O son of much inquisitiveness," I replied and passed on. Were all the guards and sentries going without their meal, I wondered. I found the ground on the way across to the fort wall difficult. My feet slid about in the hard leather shoes until I wondered how I could negotiate the sixteen miles there and back if the road was anything like the one we had travelled on to the fort. My conscience now began to trouble me. One can change one's country and one's clothes but never one's conscience! I reached the fort wall. Here, thought I, there may be one man, but there was none visible. I began to mount. The *burka* was long and stuffy, my hard shoes impossible to grip with, my hands not free. After a struggle I hoisted myself up into one of the loopholes. I had no time to reconnoitre further before a harsh loud voice shouted, "Are you so tired of this world as to want to go to the next, O daughter of a foolish mother, or do you long to be shot even as a jackal?"

"Neither," I piped in a high key, "I am in haste to carry medicine to the Chief's fort and am late now, therefore allow me to go over this wall."

By this time the man was beside me where I had dropped back on to the ground.

"You are in haste, eh, to twist your neck or your

backbone, thoughtless one? Do you think the Chief's son pays me to let senseless women such as you mount these walls? Do you want me shot for disobedience? Your neck is your own if you care so little for it, but at least my life is of value to my master, peace be upon him!"

"If I give you something to allow me to pass could you forget you had seen me?"

"Turn back to where you came from, treacherous one. I am here because my eyesight is good, and my memory long. You are not of this fort and the safe road is past the guards at the entrance. If you can pass them go your way."

By this time a knot of guards had gathered and I feared detection. The only course was to go back into the fort defeated. How could I ever get past these guards? I managed to pass into my apartments and discard the garments, and decided that better plans would have to be laid if there was to be any prospect of exploration.

That night unexpectedly the caravan returned. My chance had gone for the present. I felt depressed at the evening meal. My husband was telling me of the other fort—how there had been a raid a week ago and they were building up part of the fort wall which had been destroyed. "Some people have all the luck," I said disgustedly, and meant it.

Next day while we were having our midday meal a servant came into the room to say a messenger awaited the master of the house outside.

"Do you know it is meal-time? What messenger

can demand an interview at this time?" I asked angrily.

"It is urgent from the Chief," the man replied. My husband left the room and was away some ten minutes. When he came back he looked rather anxious and I asked him what was the matter.

"Nothing," he said. "My father wants me to go as soon as possible—that is all."

"But this afternoon we are riding to the old ruined fort!"

"I'm afraid we must put it off. This life is different from what you have been accustomed to, Morag. Things happen sometimes—things that change the whole of one's life. I hope nothing like that will ever happen to us."

"Of course not," I replied.

"I am sometimes afraid of anything happening to me, for your sake and Margaret's." He looked into the distance.

"I've never seen you so gloomy," I said, as we finished our meal.

"Morag," Syed said earnestly, "if anything happens to me at any time, always remember you can claim your dowry and if you want to go home my father will see you safely as far as Peshawar. If you choose to remain you will be safe with my people. They all like you and will protect you here. Remember always that I loved you. I must hurry now. God be with you till we meet again."

I could not understand the sadness of his tone, but he assured me nothing was wrong. A few minutes after I saw him kissing Margaret, then he ran out into the courtyard. From my window I saw the men were assembling below. A messenger rushed into the courtyard. All crowded round him. He ran out again, jumped on his horse and rode at a gallop. The horse's neck was covered with foam splashes. I called my companion. "Where are the men going?" "Only a short journey, respected one. They often go like that. Would the honoured one care to rest?"

"Yes, presently. First I shall watch the men leave."

My husband was now mounted, as were about twenty others. As he reached the gate he looked back and raised his hand in salute, and the procession moved off. I had never seen Syed armed. Moreover, surely all the men must now have left our fort. My companion was not very helpful. The guards would still be there, she said, for no fort was ever left unguarded. I sent for one of the head menservants.

"I am going to the Chief's fort and I am going alone. Get my horse."

"Honoured Begum," he said, greatly agitated, "there is to be a raid on the fort of a relation of the family. The enemy, the spies tell us, have been mustering, they have read in the stars that it is auspicious for the raid to begin to-day. The roads will not be safe any time from now. The honoured son of the Chief is even now on his way to go with his respected father."

So that was it! I felt foolish not to have thought it out for myself. What could I do? Women were not allowed to join the fray while the men were alive. I paced up and down the room and kept looking across the hills. The last thing I could imagine was a raid. Where would the fort be which was to be attacked? Did any man ever live through a raid? These questions I put again and again to the servant.

"It is the will of Allah," he replied resignedly. "Our men do not like to die under their quilts. I am old, too old."

"Go," I said.

Left alone I thought of everything possible. I had once heard or read of a man who by suddenly taking out his artificial teeth had so terrorized the head-hunters who had captured him that they had fled and his life had been spared. But I had no artificial teeth and was quite sure these men would not have been afraid of them if I had!

What I pictured in those long minutes! The possibility of my husband being killed occurred to me for the first time. My hand somehow reached my throat and caught the amulet my sister-in-law had given me "that the White Lady might always appear before a raid." The White Lady! The conical hill eight odd miles away! I ran to the tower and looked across to the White Lady's hill. Could I see her? Would she come? Perhaps. Suppose she did not! "O God," I prayed, "let something happen that this raid will not take place!"

The servants in the fort went about their duties without concern. The men left behind felt it a direct insult not to be in the fray. Again and again I thought over Syed's last words: "Remember if anything happens to me——" This would be no ordinary fight. Most of it was bound to be in the open and in daylight. It was agony to think of it. No shipwrecked mariner ever looked from his desert island for a sail as I watched for the White Lady.

It was now an hour since my husband and the men had left. Suddenly an idea came—suppose I could get to that conical hill, dressed in white, climb up and wave a white gauzy scarf! Again, suppose I met the raiders? If they were brigands they would either kill me or take me to their caves. Yet why should I meet the enemy, I thought. In any case the road would be rough, and the sooner I was away the better.

If one thought lucidly at such times one would have too much sense to act as one does. The thought uppermost in my mind was to save my husband; if any act stupid or otherwise could do it, I preferred to be stupid than to stay in the fort idle. I decided to go out on horseback and to leave the rest to chance. First, I wrote a letter to my mother-in-law:

RESPECTED ONE,

While my husband is visiting you I am going out into the hills a little way on horseback. I love the hills and am anxious to explore them. I hope to visit you to-morrow. I have told the guards I shall return in one hour.

MARGARET'S MOTHER

That, I thought, would explain my going out if anything happened to me. As I put it into the letter-box which Syed had had made for me like the one we had in Edinburgh, I wondered who would take it out!

With much expostulation the groom brought my horse. Should he not go with me?

"I shall return in an hour. I am going to gather leaves to make a medicine," I told my companion. The sentry allowed me to pass. Which road to take I did not know. The only thing I was sure of was that the sentries would watch me as far as possible. I must get quickly out of sight. The going was difficult. A bend in the road now hid the fort—I slipped from the horse and took off my riding-boots, putting on a pair of servant's slippers which I had tucked under my *burka*. I covered the boots with stones, tied the horse to a tree, and followed a narrow path which led roughly in the direction of the hill eight odd miles away. Determination alone took me over the rocky stony road. I had no watch with me. From time to time I breathed a prayer.

The road cut to the right now, up a hill. I decided to keep on ahead. Mercifully the White Lady's hill was visible and so unlike the rest that it was easy to recognize. The stuffy *burka* was hotter than anything I ever thought could be. My feet were already sore, and I would gladly have walked without shoes had not some of the stones been sharp as knives. Then I heard steps. The brigands! My heart stood still. Flight was out of the question. I closed my eyes. I would go on. Presently a villager appeared leading some oxen. "Peace be upon you," he said in passing. I nodded in reply, then looked back, to find him also looking back at me. Would he send anyone after a maid who perhaps had no right to be where I was? "Fool," I thought. "Do you not know there is to be a raid?" I wanted to run back and tell him. Was I getting near the hill? It certainly looked quite close now, yet I felt unable to go on. If only I took off the *burka*! But that would ruin everything—I must keep it on. I might manage to get there! I could now hear distant drums. Had the enemy left their fort? What did those drums mean? The White Lady had not shown herself and I had far to go yet. How many times I stumbled on that road, how many times I looked back and then to the conical hill, I know not. Just when my strength was about to give out, I became dimly aware that I had arrived. I looked round; everywhere hills seemed to hide me. Near the foot of this particular one were large boulders and scrub-like growth. I took off the *burka* and rolling it up threw it into the bush. It was like parting with a weapon in a cage of wild animals, for without it I was liable to meet with disaster.

How my feet ached! I unwrapped the gauzy material from my neck and shoulders. Drums seemed to be beating quite near, or was it only in my brain? Was this the right hill? Would my horse, left alone, make noise enough to attract the fort guards? Shouts borne from afar reached me. Were they from the fort sentries who had followed me? People say one feels inspired in such circumstances, but I certainly did not. I felt dull, stupid —wanted to run back down the hill and put on the *burka*. I began to think, as through a haze, of Syed and Margaret. The drums beat on. Steadily I walked up the hill. The shouts surely were nearer. How steep a hill it was! At each step stones rolled down. There was little foot-hold, and in some places I had to use my hands to pull myself up. Would they see me? Suppose it were the wrong hill? On I went, the hill narrowed. The drapery floated round me. I had now nearly reached the top. All around the air was cool and the breeze fluttered my veil. I felt like a ghost, aloof—in the world, yet not of it.

Did the clansmen, friend and foe, see the White Lady? Right on the very summit I stood, imagining that I would look life-size to those in the distance.

Suddenly I heard a shout that sounded near at hand. I turned to descend. A shot rang out. I heard a sound like a bullet tearing through tree foliage. More shots came. I hurried down the hill as quickly as the slipping stones allowed. Fear must be the best-known driver! If I could get into the undergrowth at the base of the hill, I would be on the sheltered side, and perhaps the hill was between the two rival clansmen, or they might be firing some warning to each other. My chief thought was to get to shelter, for if I were discovered my fate would not be enviable. I could now hear more shouts. I stumbled down the hill praying that I might reach the undergrowth in time. At last, expecting to find hidden enemies behind the boulders, I reached the foot of the hill. I had now the choice either to face what might be behind the boulders, or to have the marksman come upon me. I chose the former alternative. Luck was with me. A kind of cave was almost in front of me—I crept in. It was so dark I groped my way along the wall, and when I was well inside I stood still. It seemed to be empty, but perhaps some one was watching, waiting in the darkness. My mouth was parched and swollen. Between thirst, fear of the man who might be searching for me, and fear of what might be in the darkness behind me, I doubted if I could summon up enough courage to leave the place. Presently I heard sliding feet and falling stones, and I remembered the *burka* —would the whiteness of it attract attention? More afraid I could not be. I had got to the stage when fear begets bravery, and having no hopes of getting away, and being fully aware of some one armed being near, I crept step by step to the entrance, conscious of the risk and yet being unable to stay longer in the darkness. At the mouth of the cave I stopped; my aching feet still slipped about. I caught sight of a clansman with cartridge-belt and rifle sliding down with his back to me. If I had had a rifle I would have fired, for it would have been a case of my life or his. I must have come to the wrong hill after all, for belief in the legend was so powerful that no clansman would ever ascend it. Slowly I withdrew into the cave again, determined to watch until the man passed the mouth—supposing of course that he was the cave's rightful inhabitant. Minutes, or hours, passed. Then I saw a figure pass across the light. I bent down, but he had gone. I crept quickly to the entrance and, removing the drapery which hung about me torn and shredded, peeped out, keeping my head close against the jagged rocks. What I saw caused me to cram the veil into my mouth.

There, with his rifle on the ground while he examined the *burka*, stood Syed! His name escaped my lips. He was within five yards of me. He swung round and stood still as I ran out of the cave. The situation was absurdly unreal, for him more than for me.

"You!" he whispered.

"The brave clansman!" I teased him.

"You are real, I . . . I . . . thought it was something . . . I was seeing."

"I'm real enough. What about the raid? I thought I would never see you again."

"I did not want you to know of it. Those men watched the hill for their White Lady. I was so sick of it I got away and determined to shoot if I saw anything like a figure—knowing quite well it is only superstition. Morag, I had no idea you were here. How did you come? Who brought you? Why did you come?" His surprise was only equalled by my relief.

"There will be no holding them now they have seen the White Lady," Syed went on. "I was so amazed to see the figure, for a moment I scarcely believed my eyes. It was the solidity of it that made me guess it was alive, but I meant to hit it all the same. The raiders must have seen it too. They never appeared, although our men went out to scout. Morag, for God's sake never do that again! It would have been worse than a raid if I had shot you."

"Yes, for you," I replied.

We must have looked a peculiar pair as we trekked back to the fort. My husband was slung with cartridge-belts, knives, and rifle, while I, footsore and too weary to talk, followed behind. It must have looked like the capture of a reluctant bride.

"No word of this to anybody," said Syed, as I untied my horse and slipped my bruised feet into my riding-boots.

If the groups of excited clansmen standing about the courtyard had known the truth I wondered what they would have said. As it was, they took it as a manifestation which they believed in but did not understand.

My sisters-in-law both came next day. They were bubbling with excitement. Had I seen the White Lady? They said the clansmen were paralysed with amazement. None could now deny the truth of her appearance. "Let us pray for her soul to-night," said the younger girl. "You pray too, Bhabi Jan."

"I shall," I replied emphatically.

CHAPTER VIII

A 'FREE LAND' ENGAGEMENT

MY experience of a premeditated raid left me rather disinclined for a repetition. I felt happy in the garden where my sisters-in-law and I spent the long afternoon when we were not riding out on horseback or picnicking somewhere in the hills. The necessity of always having to take armed guards with us spoiled the chance of going off on any exploration, but such journeys nevertheless served as a means to that end. At least once each week my sisters-in-law, Selima and Halima, came to spend the day with me. They brought marvellous beauty preparations which seemed to make one attractive almost immediately, scented clinging powder and rouge which lasted all day. We hennaed our finger-nails and toe-nails, rouged our cheeks, chins, and ears, and put kohl on our eyelids, giving a dreamy look to the eyes which is very fascinating. In return I produced a pair of antiquated hair-curling tongs. The girls were more delighted with these—which they had never seen before—than with everything else put together. They heated the tongs over a charcoal brazier and waved each other's hair with more energy than efficiency, until they were obliged to fix their veils tightly at the back to keep it down! The elder of the two girls was eighteen. Her soft grey eyes sometimes looked quite blue; her face was the perfect oval so exalted by artists, her complexion almost too perfect to be true. We became great friends and she used to confide everything to me.

One day we were walking alone in the garden. I could not help wondering why such a charming girl was unmarried, and I said, "Are you not going to marry some day, Bhabi Selima?" For a few seconds she did not answer; then she said, "Yes, certainly I shall, but I must marry the son of a great chieftain. I could not marry an ordinary man. You know, our men are all warriors and they would make sport of a man who could not take his place with them."

"Of course," I replied. "There must be many chieftains here who have sons."

"There are many, but I am not going to hurry to choose one in case he may not be a good warrior. He must be handsome, dashing, brave, and yet kind. I do not think there can be many just as I want him to be."

"But surely you want only one!" I said, and we both laughed.

"Yes, you see there is only one like him—that is why it is so difficult. You know my father is very gruff and is always busy. He is very kind to us and we love him, but being such a great chieftain he is accustomed to give orders and forgets sometimes when he talks to us that we are not always a hundred yards away from him! He was very angry when he knew our brother wanted to marry outside the clan, and for days we were afraid to speak to him. He wanted to keep Syed from coming back here again, but we, my sister and I and our aunt, talked to him so much, and at last my aunt, who was your proxy mother at the wedding, made my father laugh by reminding him how he had once angered his father! We knew then that all was well. Now he is very pleased and proud of you."

The next day I spent with my mother-in-law. During my stay an elderly woman paid a visit. She spoke of the local news, walked in the rose-garden, and went away after having a number of cups of green tea. Her next visit was also paid during a few hours I spent at the fort. My mother-in-law, myself, and two aunts entertained her; the girls did not appear. The old khanum[1] visitor stayed to the midday meal and praised a pudding we had that day, made of almonds, sweetened browned flour, cream and rose-water. My mother-in-law said it was a very difficult pudding to make, and that it had been prepared by Selima, who was interested in cooking and was a splendid house-keeper. After lunch our visitor was shown Selima's embroidery and the different patterns she could work. She praised them all and went home.

"Who is this visitor?" I asked my mother-in-law.

"She is a member of a rival chieftain's clan, a woman of good repute for knowledge of household affairs, and she can keep fifty servants continually employed."

I was suitably impressed, as the old lady certainly

[1] A term meaning a lady of distinction.

seemed to awe my women-servants even more than I could.

"Do you receive the relations of rival chieftains?" I inquired.

"Certainly, except when there is a feud or a raid. But afterwards when peace is declared we visit each other again."

She paused a moment, then went on: "Our men fight fairly. We guard our forts carefully in order that we may not be dishonoured by a surprise attack. For any man who is stabbed in the back has proved himself a coward, and there is only one word in our clan law for him—'outlaw.'"

Just then I thought my mother-in-law a strange mixture of bravery and appealing femininity. She looked almost fragile as she stood silhouetted against the wall of the fort, yet one could have imagined her holding the fort with eye and hand steady as any man.

"Now I am expecting this khanum to return to-day, and I want you, Halima Begum, and Selima Begum to be in the garden near the fountain when she arrives. At a signal from me you will please ask Selima Begum to go to her apartment, while we are approaching you and your sister."

"I shall do as you desire, respected one," I replied, wondering what subtlety lay beneath her request, for the look which accompanied it, a glance half knowing, half diplomatic, was intended to convey that something of importance was afoot.

"Peace be upon you, light of my eyes; I shall now prepare to receive our guest. You may, if you care to accept it, have the hospitality of any of my clothes you think worthy of wearing."

This seemed a gentle hint to me that instead of going back to our fort to dress, as the occasion evidently demanded, I was to borrow some clothes there. As fashions happily never change one does not 'date' people by their clothes, and the older women's garments are the same as those of the younger.

My mother-in-law's veils, jumpers, and trousers were all so lovely that after the maid had put out at least thirty complete outfits I closed my eyes and put my hand on one at random. It proved to be blue, a gauzy dreamy sapphire blue, with mauve veil and gold trousers shot with sapphire blue, and a sapphire-blue jumper. The light made the sequins twinkle like stars. My mother-in-law was in pink with embroideries in black and gold. Halima Begum was in rose-pink and Selima in a fairy-like garment of sky-blue and silver. I felt when we gathered in the rose-garden round the fountain that we had no opposition to fear from the flowers!

There was a tenseness in the atmosphere. My younger sister-in-law chatted incessantly, but Selima and I were unusually restrained. She spent the time picking to pieces roses from a bush which had grown in the garden of a lovely Moghul princess in India over a century ago. I watched the archway through which my mother-in-law was to appear before giving me the signal. If a fairy prince had entered mounted on a fiery charger it would have seemed perfectly in order. I could see my father-in-law pacing, as was his custom, backwards and forwards on the battlements, pausing every now and then when something evidently puzzling occurred to him. The scene gave me the sensation of being in a medieval castle before a siege.

Presently very slowly through the archway my mother-in-law and the visitor appeared. I watched intently for the signal, but saw none. The flowers were admired, the ponds examined, the rockery and the rose arches, before my suspense was ended. Then she raised her right hand to her left shoulder and looked at me.

"Will you please go to your rooms, Selima?" I asked.

"Certainly, if you wish it, Bhabi Jan," she replied, and taking the path leading parallel to her mother, she walked with downcast head into the house. The two women waited until she had passed them, then both turned and watched her out of sight. Then Halima and I joined the other two. We talked for a little while, always allowing the guest to start a new subject, as is the etiquette, and never 'going one better.'

Tea was carried out to the walled rose-garden and we drank this and ate sweets and cakes for at least an hour, after which our visitor took her leave.

It all puzzled me considerably. On her next visit the old khanum was accompanied by several women of her own age, sisters of the rival chieftain. We had a huge lunch which took fully two hours even though one ate only a little of each dish and sipped non-intoxicant sherbet from tiny little green-and-gold-lined glasses. The feast over, we younger ones took our cue from the elders and left the room.

I began to wonder who would come with our visitor next, and was not in doubt long, for the following Friday—which is looked upon as being the most auspicious day—I received a message asking me to go again to the fort and be present to receive some important guests. There is nothing haphazard in Frontier entertaining. The people are born hosts, and their hobby, if it is not fighting, is indisputably entertaining.

I arrived punctually and was received with greatly suppressed excitement. I had dressed so that 'the hospitality of the wardrobe' would not be required, and found the other ladies equally carefully attired. My father-in-law was nowhere to be seen. I inquired for him and was told he was well but was engaged with his head villagers on important questions. Presently with considerable pomp the guests were announced. My sisters-in-law asked their mother's permission to walk in the garden. I would have liked to go too, but that was not in the Begum's plan. She at once began to speak of a merchant on his way to India who was bringing materials next day from which we were to choose new clothes, and thus she kept me talking.

By this time the ladies had entered—five of them. We stood up, I behind my mother-in-law, and bowed to the guests, who bowed in turn or kissed hands as status warranted. They seemed to be so polished, decorous, polite, and ceremonious that I, who longed only to roam the hills and explore wherever fancy led, felt like retreat. Perhaps, I thought, it might be possible, but even now the Begum was beckoning to me to be seated. The eldest lady, or the most important guest, now opened the conversation by inquiring about the health of the family. Green tea and sweets were brought, and three servants were kept busy. When we had turned our cups upside down in the saucers to denote we had finished the retainers left the room; the wife of the rival chieftain said that they were greatly honoured to pay the visit.

"My eyes," she said, "are gladdened by the sight of so much delight and gracious hospitality and also by seeing one endowed with so many great qualities from a land so far across the hills and seas."

"The honour is ours," replied my mother-in-law, "and I trust all the members of your clan are enjoying perfect health and prosperity."

"It is indeed so," continued our chief guest. "My husband the Chieftain, as you know, is a man of noted qualities and great dignity, and we are, though well in health, a little troubled by serious thoughts."

"It is with the greatest sympathy I hear of this. If it lies in my power to relieve your distress it would be a pleasure even to entertain the thought."

"Kind friends as you and the Chieftain are, I feel it my duty to put my distress of mind into your lap."

"Pray speak," replied my mother-in-law.

"My husband and I are old and begin to feel anxious as to the future of our family."

"A very natural fear, but I trust your family is in good health," said the hostess with feeling.

"My daughters are not my greatest fear—they are endowed with many good qualities and are housekeepers of unusual merit and not unpleasing to the eye."

"Indeed, your daughters are most delightful girls and as beautiful as early dew on roses."

The rival chieftain's wife bowed gracefully in acknowledgment of the compliment.

"My great trouble is my son."

"You have a son then, Begum Sadaat?"

Here I should add that the expression of assumed surprise was intended to create a delicacy in the situation; for of course every one present knew the facts.

"Most assuredly, a fine lad of twenty-two, brave as any in the land," she remarked, heightening the drama. "He can shoot with the best, but is wayward of thought and action. I greatly desire that he should become a more responsible young man."

"Can it be my pleasure to assist in any way?" inquired my mother-in-law.

"Well, you know my son is the heir to vast lands and an honourable name, and will be a great chief one day himself. I had just thought that if you might agree to give it your consideration, my son might enter into the slavery of your daughter, Selima Begum!"

The khanum looked away for a moment in thought. "This of course is a question which will require much discussion with my husband the

Chief. If, however, you will do us the honour of presenting yourself next Friday, we shall be in a position to have the honour of relieving your anxiety on the subject."

"It will be an honour to present ourselves on the day you have selected," replied the anxious Begum Sadaat, and rose to leave.

The ceremony of this proposal appeared to have been unpremeditated. No onlooker, however shrewd, would have guessed that this affair had been discussed for practically six months, and was following the usual course that 'Free Land' etiquette demands!

The ladies parted with great ceremony. The fact that this marriage would join the two most courageous and powerful clans in the land was not a thing they showed, even if they felt it. I could imagine what it must have meant to these two women, whose men had fought and died in many a raid against each other, sitting calmly discussing what amounted to a permanent cessation of hostilities between their clans! They might have been comparing their households with nothing more at stake than the price of tea and sugar.

The guests now left, and I accompanied the khanum to my father-in-law's business-room. The old Chieftain was writing, and we stood for a few moments until he greeted us. "Peace be upon you! I am busy at the moment."

"And upon you be peace," his wife replied. "I have just had some visitors."

"Yes? I trust the visit has been a pleasant one."

"Very. Our guests were much pleased with their reception."

"Is it new that people should be glad to be received in our fort? Does our hospitality lack warmth?" asked the Chieftain, in a tone that allowed of no argument.

"On the contrary, honoured one," soothingly replied his wife, "our hospitality is ever the best these hills afford, and becoming to the dignity of our guests."

"That is as it ought to be. And now I must not detain you ladies longer."

"If we are not disturbing you?"

"Well, I am busy and our conversation is over," replied the Chieftain.

"I would speak to you on important matters, if your time permits—about our daughter Selima Begum."

"What ails the girl?"

"Nothing, but with your permission we may announce her engagement to the son of Chieftain of the Killa Fort!"

"Chieftain of the Killa Fort! Does he think his son is a match for my daughter? Have we not always driven them back in battle and will——"

"Certainly," my mother-in-law interposed. "Our daughter, as they know, belongs to a greatly superior clan; they agree that you are without doubt the greatest warrior and ours the clan to be most feared in the land."

Thus mollified, the Chieftain waved his hand. "Do not interrupt me with these trivial affairs.

Marry our daughter to the brave son of a fearless man. I have never noticed he showed signs of retreat until his ammunition was finished and sword-hand useless. It is a pity, for he was a man worth fighting! Peace be upon you!"

He sat down again; the interview was over. As I followed the khanum back to our apartments I wondered whether the old Chieftain, like his wife, was a master at hiding his emotion.

It was a relief to me to hear of the engagement, for the bridegroom-elect was the brother of the girl whom the old Chieftain had chosen for Syed, and I always felt conscious that, but for me, these two powerful clans would have been already united.

Surely, I thought, the ceremony of the engagement was now over, but it was not. The following Friday a procession arrived in the courtyard headed by a striking figure in a wonderfully tied turban and mounted on a perfect horse. The rider sat as upright as a statue, holding the reins with his right hand, while his left hand rested on the hilt of his glittering sword. Drums and other musical instruments brought up the rear.

My sisters-in-law and I were sitting on the balcony. "There he is," said Selima Begum. "He is splendid and brave, I am sure. Do you not think so, Bhabi Jan?"

"I am sure he is," I replied.

"The son of the Chief of the Killa Fort!" said my younger sister-in-law in whispered awe. "How glad we shall be, my sister, when these two clans fight no more."

An Everyday Scene in a 'Free Land' Fort

"Yes, thanks be to Allah, our clan aided by theirs will be greatly feared," replied Selima Begum.

Greetings were being exchanged in the courtyard below, something like those indulged in by the two khanums in the pre-engagement days.

My sisters-in-law, their mother, and all the women-servants now gathered on the balcony, each one peeping out as far as she could in order not to miss any detail of what was happening. All acclaimed the handsomeness, brave looks, and dignified bearing of the young man.

Selima's cheeks were pink with excitement. She had never looked so pretty, with her eyes twinkling with the joy of being the cause of so much pleasure.

This visit proved to be but another excuse for a feast which the kitchen had no doubt prepared for. No restaurant could have turned out such roast chickens, pilaus, and roast lambs as appeared half an hour later.

Selima and I peeped round the corner of a curtain leading to the men's dining-rooms and had a good look at the bridegroom-elect. He was as handsome as distance had made him out to be, and as Selima clasped her hands and laughed into them I knew there would be peace in future between these two clans.

Next day the khanum from the Killa Fort came again. This time she uncovered two lengths of beautiful material, one red and one green. "To make a garment for Selima Begum," she said. My mother-in-law took the green. This meant the acceptance of the engagement; had the red been taken it would have denoted refusal.

The news travelled, presents began to arrive, people came to pay their respects and wish happiness to the betrothed pair. Maids sewed day and night, while the girls and I talked of the new fort Selima Begum would go to and how we would visit her.

The following day the one-time rivals met. I was specially anxious to witness the way they agreed to forget the past. Selima, her mother and sister, and I gathered on our balcony, until excitedly we heard the arrival at the gateway. The fort was beflagged, and every man had tied his turban as rakishly as a turban can be tied. All the best there was in the fort was on view. The gates opened, and in came the party, well armed as usual, headed by the Chieftain of the Killa Fort, grim as though bent on attack. My father-in-law, every bit as forbidding, stood rigid within the courtyard. Had I been the visiting chieftain I would have felt relieved to claim this giant of six feet six inches as my friend! Within a few feet of my father-in-law the Chieftain dismounted and stood still. "Peace be upon you, great Chief," he saluted.

"And upon you too," my father-in-law replied, continuing, "I welcome you here to-day and am proud to do so, for you were ever a gallant foe. As boys we fought, as young men we fought, now as old men we become friends. Clansmen, salute our new ally, the great Chief of Killa Fort!" Two volleys rang out. My father-in-law stepped forward, placed his head on the right shoulder of his former foe, then on the left. The Khan of Killa gave the same greeting. Cheer upon cheer rose in the air, tears ran down our faces. Hollywood has never produced so moving a scene. The Chieftain led the way to the feast. We dried our tears; there was no necessity for any more.

CHAPTER IX

THE WOMEN DEFEND THE FORT

AFTER Selima Begum's engagement was announced thrill followed thrill. Presents arrived in a continuous stream. The news that two powerful clans were now friends caused mixed feelings. There were those who were glad, and those who no doubt had cause to be less so. The presents from the bridegroom-elect's people were composed of everything from humble household cooking-utensils to exquisite jewellery. The clothes alone would have been sufficient for fifty brides and then might well have caused comment, for every clanswomen gives at least one garment to a newly engaged girl.

Gifts were sent to the bride's *fiancé*, and news was spread of the marvellous saddles, guns, heaps of gold tomans,[1] ammunition, *tulwars*, and swords. The most wonderful gift was a perfect Arab horse, supposed to be the finest specimen ever seen and greatly desired by all. The owner, an uncle of the Chief of Killa Fort, was old and wanted to see the horse disposed of as he desired before his death.

Invitations came for the womenfolk of our clan to go to Killa Fort to a feast in honour of the occasion and by thus 'eating the salt,' as it is called, to show we were reconciled and friendly.

[1] Toman=£1 English.

We packed all our smartest clothes, our best gold slippers and jewellery, and were to leave in three days. These days were crowded with excitement. Messengers were arriving with orders from my father-in-law the Chief's fort, while our own messengers were continually on the run with our replies. There must be no hitch in these preparations, no cause for the clan's name to be ridiculed! I was afraid some quite innocent act of mine—as this was my first experience—might give displeasure, but my mother-in-law with her unfailing diplomacy supervised all my endeavours to do my best, and for two afternoons put me through the different salutations to be given to the clanswomen when we met. Each night instead of going to sleep I rigged up in my bedroom an imitation reception-hall, with boxes against the wall representing Killa Fort clanswomen, and practised until I was salutation-perfect. Being the son's wife I came after his mother in status, and my being a *ferungi* (Englishwoman) made it even more important that I should avoid mistakes.

At last the day of the departure came. Our luggage would have taken us twice round the world. My mother-in-law went first on horseback, I followed, behind came the excited Selima Begum and her sister. Armed guards were in front, behind, and on both sides. An hour before we left a bonfire was lighted so that the Killa Fort people might know of our departure. No sooner had its smoke been seen by them than they lit an answering fire on their hill. We left in great style, being given a salute by the clansmen, and I thought of the difference between this leisurely going and my hurried and surreptitious exit the day I negotiated the road to the White Lady's hill on feet cut by the sharp stones.

The three-hour journey passed without mishap, and our arrival at the Killa Fort was welcomed with a salvo in which every man must have joined. Bunting was everywhere, strings of roses and cut-paper foliage in all colours made by the deft-fingered villagers. Some one with more than the ordinary love of gaiety had even stuffed coloured paper into the loopholes.

We dismounted and were shown at once into the women's apartments, which were hung with decorations. At the door of the reception-hall the Khanum of the Killa Fort received us. She was past middle age, with greyish hair, fine eyebrows shading soft brown eyes, and had given much thought to her clothes, but I think not more than we had given to ours! From head to foot she was dressed in gold shot with shimmering blue and pink. Her little gold cap was massed with small artificial roses, and over it her sparkling golden veil hung gracefully.

"Welcome and peace be upon you, bearer of so honourable a name," she began. "On this great occasion it is my pleasant duty to be, by the will of Allah, well in health to give you welcome suitable to your clan. The honour is all the greater on account of your respected daughter and the wife of your noble son, who comes to share our gladness of heart. To her too we give greetings." My mother-in-law bowed, I followed with the same salutations.

"Peace be upon you, the scion of so worthy an

ally. It gives me the greatest pleasure to join you in this feast of welcome. May Allah give us all his blessing!" With a low bow my mother-in-law walked into the room towards a group of girls and women. I bowed twice and then kissed the hand of the khanum; she then kissed my forehead and I passed next into the room. Selima Begum and her sister followed with greetings first to the khanum, who joined us as I reached the group. Then followed introductions, brow-kissing, hand-kissing, curtseying, and more hand-kissing from the youngest girls, and we were taken to our apartments. From our balcony we could see the bonfire at my father-in-law's fort, and below in the courtyard great displays of shooting, jumping, and wrestling between the men of the Killa Fort clan. Our clansmen were not with us. It is customary for only the women to attend the engagement feast.

Servants were supplied—four to each of us—to wait upon us, dress our hair, and assist us to dress. They put scent on my wrists and behind my ears, a thin film of the secret face-powder, a little rouge—and all four vowed they had never seen such perfection. The other maids in the other rooms were probably saying just the same to my relations! My sisters-in-law certainly looked lovely. There were fifteen girls there to welcome us, daughters of the fort and nieces from a fort some ten miles distant. We feasted for quite two hours, during which the two khanums paid each other compliments, saying practically the same thing in different ways.

After the feast we girls were allowed to exchange

confidences in our own rooms; we gave each other charms, heard the latest the stars foretold for us and the speculations made for the future fort of Selima Begum, and looked at each other's jewellery. I was asked many questions about my country. They could not believe the stories about the traffic and said the policemen must really be magicians if they succeeded in keeping so many cars and people going in the same direction without being killed by the dozen! They marvelled at the description of the shops and at Western women being allowed to mix with men shoppers who dared to look at other men's wives! Nothing, they all agreed, would persuade them to travel in an aeroplane, which their clansmen called a "devil machine" and which must have been invented by "the Devil." Among them I began to feel almost as much handicapped as the man who was suddenly shot into the country of the blind. I had to unlearn a great deal, and quickly.

After the evening meal we were sitting on the balcony sipping sherbet and eating sweets when we saw a stranger arrive. He was a travelling blacksmith with veterinary skill who examined horses' feet and treated them if they required it. He produced references from other surrounding chiefs speaking of his abilities and was at once engaged to go the round of the horses in the Killa Fort. He seemed a very efficient and painstaking man and would not even leave his work to go to the evening meal, saying he preferred to work until finished and then to travel on, as he had to reach another fort before nightfall. The men left him, praising his skill, and were in the midst of their meal when we heard a furious galloping, and running out on to our balcony we saw a fast-disappearing horse and rider at full gallop. The guards fired, the watchman shouted, "The Arab! The Arab!" The courtyard was full of excited, half-stupefied men. The guards exclaimed that the blacksmith had galloped past when they were unprepared, for as it was meal-time only half of their number were on duty. Who was the blacksmith? Which direction did he take? Questions were called without being answered. The men were now mounted and rallied outside the courtyard. The Chief of the Killa Fort was directing twenty men in one direction, twenty in another, and so on. Sending farewells to his wife and daughters he galloped off and disappeared from sight. The sound of galloping horses, the *thud*, *thud*, peculiar to that part filled the air. We were astounded at the unexpectedness of the event. Standing there as darkness began to fall we watched in vain for the return of either clansmen or Arab, or both. At bed-time they were still absent and we decided to lie down on our beds and rest. The excitement of the day and now the anxiety overcame us. It was a sorry end to the engagement feast. I lay awake wishing the men would return. Suppose they were set upon by hill-brigands and killed, shot by men who knew the hills perhaps better than they and who would take their lives for the guns and ammunition they carried, and counting themselves in luck would ride off to their fastnesses. I got up and hastily wrote a note to my husband:

> The Arab has been stolen. The Killa Fort clansmen left hours ago to search. Am afraid something has happened. For heaven's sake have help sent.

Calling a servant I asked for this to be sent immediately to my father-in-law's fort, where Syed was staying during my absence. With relief I heard the gate open and the man clatter away along the hill road. The feeling of foreboding depressed me. I went to Margaret's room—she and her nurse were both sound asleep. Tiptoeing to Selima's room I saw she was praying—I crept away. Would the daylight ever come? Would the men ever come back again? Why had none of the parties returned? Had they been ambushed? It was now eleven o'clock. Perhaps the men were back after all, I comforted myself. I would have one more look and go to bed. This was a strange country with strange ways and I was a coward, I thought. Stepping out on to the balcony I was surprised to hear distant rumblings of thunder. A flash of lightning gashed the darkness, rain poured in torrents, but through the storm I caught the sound of the crack of shots. Thank heaven! It must be the returning clansmen.

But our guards, snipers, and sentries suddenly replied. Orders flashed quick as the lightning. To the loopholes! Selima Begum was beside me.

"A raid, Bhabi Jan! The clansmen are away. There are only a few men left. Can you shoot?"

"Yes."

"I'll bring my rifle. Get yours, and as much ammunition as you can," she said quietly and slipped away.

Running in, I brought out my rifle and two belts of cartridges, which every one carries. The storm was terrific. The raiders must have been soaked through. How many were closing in on us in that awful darkness? The lightning flashed repeatedly, the thunder rumbled and crashed, every now and again the flashes caught the barrels at the loopholed wall. My sisters-in-law and the girls who could shoot joined us. There was no fear shown. Through my mind went the letter of the Chief of our clan to his son in Edinburgh: "Would she be able to defend the fort if required?" The fear was banished; my clan was as courageous as this or any other!

"Let's get to the loopholes," some one said. Selima, the elder girl, led the way. The shots drew nearer; to judge by the fusilade there must have been at least a hundred attackers. Our replies were weak. "Each to a loophole and remember the honour of your clan," called Halima Begum as we found our loopholes.

The rain was not so heavy, but the storm continued. The flashes glinted on the knives and rifles of the men approaching. The girls fired steadily and determinedly. The lightning showed the raiders crawling like snakes to the fort wall. Once they reached it, our poor defence would not hold long. Shouts and groans of the wounded outside the fort began to reach us. Our few snipers inside the walls would soon be overcome. Suddenly fierce yells rent the air. I felt like flight back to my room, but the girls held firm. This was probably our last hour in any case, nothing seemed to matter. The hand-to-hand fighting outside was furious, yells followed yells; by the lightning flashes we saw men struggling together, but our snipers inside the walls who were practically our last defence were mercifully still at their posts. There had been a check, and the whirling fighting mass seemed to me to be retreating. Another flash showed men lying on the ground. I crept to Selima Begum's side. "There is a check, the Killa Fort clansmen must have returned, and attacked the enemy's rear." Then my recollection of the note to my husband! It must be our clansmen who had come to help search for the Killa Fort men and the Arab! My husband must be out there in that nightmare scene. I must go. The suspense inside was terrible—I doubted that anyone could survive that hand-to-hand fight. I stumbled in the darkness down to the courtyard clutching my rifle and cartridge belts, but the sentry would not allow me to pass. Climbing through a window I got to the women's open courtyard. The storm was over, darkness was now blacker than ever. Shots were flying in all directions, bullets whizzed past my head. I crept, as I thought, round to the front gate of the fort. The snipers were calling, "They retreat, they retreat." I ran back fearful of what would be carried through the gate. Thankful for the mercy of the darkness, I groped my way back to the loopholed wall. The girls had heard the call passed round and were now showing signs of restrained anxiety as to who had been wounded. "Wounded," I thought. "What about the killed?" Who could have survived such a raid? The fort gates were now open. Flares were lighted and lanterns held high as men were carried through.

Shouts of victory rang through the air. I stood looking on the scene from inside a doorway on the ground-floor. They were carrying the wounded to the men's big dining-hall. My teeth chattered. I found I was still grasping the cartridge-belts.

"Dead," a man said as four clansmen passed carrying an inert figure. "He was a great warrior. God is great, on Him the salute!"

How long the weird procession lasted I did not know. I felt as though all my life had been spent watching the terrifying spectacle. Two men walking now I recognized as from our fort. I wanted to call, but no word would come. My husband must be there! But where? I crept round to the archway near the dining-hall where I could see each man being carried in. My eyes glued themselves to the passing figures.

My sisters-in-law and the other women now came down, unveiled as was their privilege in the circumstances, and walked into the dining-hall. I followed. They began to attend to the wounded men. Friend and foe lay side by side. The dead were carried to another room. Bowls of water were brought and rolls of cloth. No preference was shown to any; each man took his turn. Some lay unconscious, others called for water. I walked among them looking for a face I feared to see. Why had I sent that note?

"You help me here, light of my eyes," came my mother-in-law's voice. Daylight came and we were relieved by other women. The dead were buried. Many still lay out where they had fallen.

It turned out that my husband had not been present at the fight, having been away at another fort. His father had sent for him, but luckily by the time he arrived the enemy was retreating.

The Killa Fort clansmen were dangerous foes, yet merciful to their enemies. The raid was forgotten as they helped the wounded on their homeward way. The seriously hurt were afterwards collected by their friends.

Later we discovered that the blacksmith was not a blacksmith at all, but a notorious outlawed brigand chief, who had stolen the Arab as a ruse, so that the defenders of the Killa Fort might be weakened during the resulting search and he and his men might attack the fort for rifles and ammunition. They had been attacked and routed from the rear by the returning Killa Fort men, who in turn were aided by our clansmen arriving to help in the search for the Arab.

The horse found its own way back to the fort of the bridegroom-elect's old uncle, and had to be presented with ceremony once again.

CHAPTER X

ADVENTURE IN THE SNAKE VALLEY

WE returned next evening from celebrating the engagement feast slightly shaken from our experiences of the raid. Back in the safety of our own fort it was soon forgotten. There may be something in the air of the 'Free Land,' or something in the feeling of inevitability, but impressions seem to pass away quickly. In any case, we were so busily employed getting Selima Begum's new home in order that there was time for nothing else. We took roses from my garden and from the girls' home garden, and soon the once-neglected two acres were unrecognizable.

Until the marriage three months later we attended one fort after another where feasts were given. Sometimes my father-in-law spent a few days at our fort. On such occasions he dropped much of his gruff exterior manner and played with our little daughter, while at night, after she had gone to bed, he used to relate stories of past forays and peace-makings.

The elders among the clansmen are adepts at story-telling. They get practice during the long winter nights when in the hours before bedtime whole families gather in the living-room; outside a deathly silence reigns, and the little villages are completely cut off from one another by the deep snow. Then are told tales of the bravery not only of fellow-clansmen but of enemies in a tight corner. These Pathans seem devoid of fear. "All is according to the plan of Allah, whose ways are wonderful," they would say when anyone had a specially remarkable escape from death. They never referred to luck. Once I said, "That was lucky." "That was the will of Allah, my time is not yet," the story-teller replied. "I will tell you the story of a chieftain who feared not Allah and what became of him."

The old warrior drew himself up, arranged himself more comfortably, surveyed the group, and began his tale, which I repeat in full because it led to an adventure of my own.

"Some twenty years ago before my hair became grey and my beard had grown to the respectful length it has attained to-day, our caravans travelled much to the city of Peshawar, where the produce of our land was sold. Sheep-skins, embroidered coats and waistcoats, and other merchandise brought much money to us. Several khans' caravans joined ours and we acted as a protection to each other against robbers, who sometimes, if great resistance was shown, killed the hill-men without any pangs of conscience. One day we were joined by a wealthy Afghan merchant taking rugs to Peshawar. At a particularly lonely spot we were fired upon and unceremoniously commanded to stop. Twenty men closed in on us from all directions. Blood is hot when one is young and we aimed at them, bidding the older men keep behind the caravan. A bullet knocked the gun from my hands and I was too stupefied to do anything. The bandits surrounded us, tied us up, and drove off with the horses, leaving us with but two mules to get home. To proceed was useless. The robbers threatened to throw over the precipices any who offered resistance, and taking our money they loosed our bonds and told us to be gone, warning us that if they came across us again any time that day they would show us no mercy. We were thankful to get away with our lives and returned home with neither money nor merchandise. News after this came regularly of rich merchants being held up and killed if any resistance was offered, and it became a necessity to arm oneself well and travel in a good-sized company in order to have a measure of protection. Again we were held up some months later by the same men, now forty in number. Again we returned home, this time wounded and once more without money. Something had to be done. The elders of the village met to discuss the matter and put their ideas before the khans. Scouts were to be sent out to track the marauders and find out where they lived, and a massed raid was to be made upon them. The news spread round the hills and offers of help came from far distances. Here we had to show the length of our beards,[1] for might not foes in league with the freebooters lead us to our destruction? We laid our plans with great care and forethought. We heard

[1] Common sense.

from the scouts that the robbers occupied a disused stronghold some miles over the hills in what was called the Snake Valley. Later news was brought that the head of these robbers, who called himself 'Gulam the undefeated,' was an outlaw chief who had carried off his neighbour's daughter, deserted his fort, and taken to the hills—where he is to this day if he still lives. Maybe his hair is grey even as my own, and wisdom may have come to him and perhaps penance as well—who knows? The raid then was planned. The stars were propitious and we set out. We were a goodly gathering of trained fearless men, two hundred in all. Among us were the ten sons of my neighbour, a gallant chieftain. We were to proceed cautiously during the night, and hide if possible through the day. So great a number seen in daytime would have caused news of our approach to precede us. That night we kept a good look-out for snipers, for these men are difficult to dislodge from behind the boulders; they shoot to kill and never miss, and can go for days on a handful of dried fruit. There are gullies in these hills where several regiments might well hide unobserved. We always tried to get into one of these, and arrived that evening within a few miles of our enemy. Three of our scouts crept away and returned some hours later to say there appeared to be but three sentries on duty. All gave the same report, but were greatly alarmed as to the prospects of the attack. It was said the chief was a snake-worshipper, and that he and his men lived on the reptiles, praying all the while to Satan and receiving power from him. This seemed believable as—the story went—no caravan had ever been able to kill one of the raiders, who had many times been outnumbered. 'Why, then, did they require to raid the caravans if they could get all they wanted by praying to Satan?' some one asked. Well, we were told that the robber chief had promised Satan that in return for the strength given to overcome travellers and make him and his followers proof against bullets, he in return would kill as many of the believers in Allah as he could. At this news many of our party became afraid, not of the attack or death, but of the power of the Devil.

"The elder men talked to them, putting to shame their disbelief in the power of Allah. This somewhat pacified them, but they would not throw aside their fears. When the dawn broke some of our servants who had been watching from the boulders behind the fort returned to say they had witnessed some weird ritual in which men danced round a whirling column of what appeared to be snakes, while others ran round with rope-like things—presumably snakes—twisted round their arms. These reports were now believed by all, even by some who had previously refused to credit them.

" 'The unbeliever! The forgotten of Allah! The son of an evil father!' were exclamations heard on every side. What was to be our next move, we wondered, as we munched dried apricots and walnuts and drank from our water-bottles? The decision was that as that day was the one on which the caravans generally passed, and as in all probability the heathenish dance of the Devil-worshippers was a prelude to an attack, we should fall upon them while they were plundering.

"We were now some two miles from the road and could hear passers-by singing to steady their ebbing courage. We lay concealed for about two hours, and then the scouts reported that the robbers were assembling. We moved on, hiding as much as possible behind a conveniently overhanging shoulder of the rock. Holding our guns ready for action we awaited news from the scouts that the robbers were nearing us. Their fastness in the hills had surely never been found before, for they sent no snipers ahead as a precaution. We would take them unawares on the march.

"'Ready' passed from mouth to mouth as we heard the songs of the approaching robbers, and before we knew what had happened they had trooped down and were beneath us. With a cry of '*Allah ho Akbar* [God is great]' we fell upon them. The presence of the ladies makes the describing of that fight an indelicacy, but Satan or no, our bullets were rolling the robbers down the hill. By the beard of the Holy Pir [Saint], it was the protection of Allah that saved us, for the attack was so unexpected that the robbers had not time to draw their knives before they were dead. The robber chief stood the onslaught well and called for mercy, which we grudgingly gave, for fain would we have made the road safe without doubt for our caravans, but the man was badly wounded and had lost his weapons. Easy would it have been to have killed him, but there is no chivalry in murdering a defenceless man. 'We of the Koh Clan,' I said to him, 'will spare your life. Look around and see now not peaceful travellers lying dead by the bullets of your own men, but friends of those very men themselves. To kill you would be the work of a second. Have you ever given your victims time to say their prayers?'

" 'No!'

" 'We will drive you bound before us to your fort; your remaining men are bound likewise; some of our clansmen will stay with the wounded lest any trick be played, with orders to shoot if they suspect treachery. As we approach the fort call out for your men to bring their arms to lay before us and let us come to some arrangement suitable to us all. Either that or we shoot you dead now.'

" 'The snakes will kill you if you come to my fort!' replied the rogue.

" 'We are armed and can deal with these even as we dealt with your followers. Do you walk ahead! Your men may walk within our ranks, and with your life you shall pay if you try any of your tricks.'

"The story had it that the wives and daughters kept the fort during the men's absence, and we relied on this. We marched towards the half-disused fort, the weird stories of which had spread throughout the Frontier land and terrified the most God-fearing men whether they showed it or not.

"The bandit shot looks of hatred at us during the march back. His eyes held all the evil in the hills, and he repeated what sounded like incantations, which none of us understood. As we neared the fort we called a halt. I gave orders for one of our men to investigate whether there were other brigands within. He returned with two men to say the fort was deserted, except for two men whom he found asleep inside the courtyard. There were no snakes to be seen. We captured many guns and much ammunition; we also took the knives from the robbers and then made them show us the entire fort. We examined the whole fort with the exception of a room where the women-folk had rushed in fear. Then we marched the chief out and gave him the choice between death or becoming a Muslim. He chose the latter course, repeating '*La illa ha illalla Mohammed Rasulalah.* [There is no God but Allah, and Mohammed is his Prophet].' So we took leave of him, after having made all the surviving robbers Muslims too!

"There were no more raids on caravans. Whether the heathen robber became a good Muslim or not, we never heard of him again, and—as I have said —if he is still alive no doubt his beard is too long to admit of any foolishness. *Allah ho Akbar.*"

The story of the Koh Chief made me long to visit the Snake Valley. I felt sure the tale had become a legend and that the clansmen, being superstitious, must have imagined a good deal of it. I made up my mind to go to the fort and see the Muslimized robber if he were still alive, and, if not, at least the deserted fort was worth a visit.

Judiciously I asked the direction of this fort.

Much ingenuity had to be practised, as it would not serve my purpose to arouse suspicion which would have ended any hopes of the journey.

From what I could gather from Syed's uncle, the old Chieftain, the fort lay about ten miles away. Six of these were fairly easy going, the remaining four difficult. Some excuse for my absence for a whole day must be given, and I determined to confide in Selima Begum, who was now married and living in her new home. We chose a day on which none of her family was to visit her; I was to leave early in the morning ostensibly to spend the day with her. I took the most easily managed guard and left soon after daybreak. My husband was very anxious that I should return before darkness fell, and I could not help wondering what would have been his surprise had I told him my real destination.

The road was rough and after an hour the guard began to show signs of anxiety about the direction in which we were going.

"Only hills and robbers this way," he said.

"Are you afraid of being an hour's ride from the fort?"

"No, your Honour, I have no fear, but my master will hold me responsible for your safety, and I fear robbers may be somewhere in these hills."

"Even robbers will not kill a woman. Next time I shall bring a guard with more courage."

This had the desired effect, and my only difficulty lay as to which was 'a direct line' from where I was. Away in the distance was a peculiarly shaped wood in the form of an L. Remembering that this had been mentioned as lying in front of the robbers' fort, I determined to make for it, hoping to keep it in view.

Fearing my hill sense was not much use, I told the guard we were going to this wood. He remarked that it was a considerable distance and that deep ravines lay between which might be difficult for the horses. I replied that if we could not cross them we could always return. For an hour we negotiated a very deep ravine and had to dismount and climb up the other side. The guard took both horses and left me free to use my hands. At the top we rested —I ate sandwiches and drank water. The next half-hour we rode over a fairly level part. We seemed far from any kind of habitation, and the hill scenery changed but little.

"Are you sure you know the way back, Asaf Khan?"

"Of a surety, and I shall be glad if your Honour gives the permission to return, for I shall have to be responsible for whatever happens."

"Yes, we are only going a little beyond that wood to see the country."

"Your Ladyship may not have heard of the Snake Valley which lies in this direction?"

"I have heard of it, but how can there be snakes here? This is not Hindustan!"

"Your Honour, my brother and I are the sons of a warrior who once raided the Snake Valley with my respected master's uncle."

"And did they see any snakes?"

"At a distance, yes, but when they approached, no!"

"Of course not. Have we seen any snakes in these last hours?"

"No, your Honour, but we are not in that part yet."

"How far are we from these snakes, then?"

"I fear we are too near to them, your Honour."

"Not near enough to see them yet, and I am not afraid of anything unless I see it, and sometimes not then," I replied, angry that he should show fear already. "I thought you Pathans were not afraid of anything."

"Nor are we, your Honour, but there is evil in these parts and for that reason nobody comes near."

"Why be afraid of robbers, then? And I am told this brigand chief became a Muslim. He is probably dead now, and perhaps deserted that fort twenty years ago lest he be killed after discovery."

"Who knows, your Honour? I can but fear these reptiles whose sting is death."

"Are you so afraid of death, then?"

"No, your Honour, not of death, but of an evil death."

"I am not afraid either," I replied, ignoring the last part of his sentence. "So let us go on. I have a charm against snakes, evil, and robbers!"

"Praise be to Allah, on whom the salute," he said. "I pray it may not be required."

"All the better if it is. Only then can one judge it."

Eventually we neared the L-shaped wood and kept round the outside, following to what was probably the top of the L. Here again the hills opened out, and high up in the distance we saw a fort.

"Is that the place? Yonder?"

"Yes, your Ladyship. Allah alone knows the truth of it."

"I shall go and call on the Chief's wife, as a visitor, and to a woman surely they will offer hospitality," I said.

"We shall be eaten by snakes, your Honour, and that is no death for good Muslims."

"I have never even heard of snakes which eat human beings, unless these are different. We shall take perhaps an hour and a half to reach the place. If any questions are asked, remember we are travelling to another fort, and ask to allow our horses to rest and to drink water."

"Allah be our guide, and if I fail in my duty to take your Honour safely back to the fort of my respected master, may I perish."

"We are not going to perish and must hasten lest we do not return by nightfall."

The silence of the next part of the journey was unbroken. The horses were thirsty and foam-splashed, as though they had galloped twenty miles. The guard said this was through the fear that horses felt at approaching danger.

Suddenly we came upon the fort, which certainly looked deserted. Slowly we approached the gateway. The gates stood open. We entered and made our way to the inner courtyard. Here on the ground we saw a disreputable gipsy-like man.

"Peace be upon you," I said. "Can we rest our horses here for an hour and have water?"

The man did not reply, but scuttled away into the house, kicking off his shoes at the doorway. A few minutes later he returned with an unveiled woman-servant, shrivelled like a piece of tree-bark. Two elderly menservants followed.

"Peace be upon you," the woman called.

"And upon you too be peace! May we rest here for an hour? We are travellers and require water and rest for our horses?"

"Of a certainty." This welcome sounded slightly forced, I thought, but no doubt the woman did not see many strangers. It struck me that if she lived on snakes it was by no means a beautifying diet.

As the guard helped me to alight, he begged me not to stay nor even to go into the fort.

"Keep these horses where we can get them easily and yourself where you can see a signal from me," I said quietly and followed the woman. There was no opportunity to say more as she was beside me.

The corridors we went through were dirty and piled with pieces of old harness, sheep-skins, fruit sacks with tops folded half-way down, and old clothing hung on great nails in the wall. The old woman muttered to herself all the way. She led me through passage after passage, then up a short rickety staircase; motioning me to stand still, she went inside a room and closed the door. Outside where I stood was certainly cleaner but the quantities of old clothes about was amazing.

One part of the folding-door opened and the

woman beckoned me in. Passing into the room I noticed the same confusion. The oppressiveness of the place seemed to catch my breath. At first no one was to be seen, but as my eyes grew accustomed to the gloom I saw a woman lying on a low bed in one corner.

She put up her hand to shade her eyes as she looked at me.

"Peace be upon you!" Her voice was irritable and sounded old and cracked.

"Peace be upon you too! I am sorry to be obliged to ask hospitality, but I and my guard are travelling to a far fort and are thirsty."

"Bring water," she said to the maid. I removed my *burka*.

When we were left alone the woman said:

"We see few people here. It is many years since I saw a visitor. I have three old women-servants."

"You must feel lonely," I ventured. "Are you ill?"

"Thanks be to Allah, no! I am in good health, and I prefer to be alone."

This did not seem to be much of a welcome. I noticed the suffocating atmosphere was due to the tightly closed window high in the wall and a small lamp burning underneath it. The floor was simply earth-swept, and there was no furniture of any kind in the room.

"You speak not our tongue with speed, O stranger. Are you of these hills?"

"I am living in these hills, but come from a land beyond the sea."

"What word is that you say—'sea'? Of what do you speak?"

"Have you not heard of the sea?"

"No. Is it in the land of the *ferungis*?"

"There is sea at Karachi in India."

"It may be they need these things. We need them not. But tell me, have you a husband?"

"Yes, I have."

"Is he a *ferungi* that he allows you to walk abroad?"

"No, he is not an Englishman."

"Are you one of the free women of Circassia?" (These women go unveiled.)

"No, I am a Muslim."

"Never have I seen your like; maybe you are an *afrit* [spirit] and have come to destroy me."

"Why should I destroy you when I seek your hospitality?"

"Perhaps not, then. Do you know who I am?"

"I know nothing of your clan."

"I was a beautiful maiden, more beautiful than the new moon, and fell in love against the wishes of my father with a neighbouring chief. Do you know the Alif Fort?"

"No."

"That was ours. I fled with the Chief, thus starting a blood-feud with a dozen clans and more of my relations, and we escaped here, where we have lived these twenty years."

Could this old hag be the beautiful maiden? Could she be the wife of the Muslimized robber?

"My beauty is such that my husband cares not for me to leave this room, lest the *afrits* see me and are jealous. Do you not think my eyes are as the dawn of morning?"

"Yes, indeed."

No wonder, I thought, this unfortunate woman looked as she did, if for twenty years she had lived in these circumstances. She could not have been more than forty, if the story were true, and yet she might have been seventy, so wrinkled was her face. It was perhaps lucky there appeared to be no looking-glasses anywhere.

The servant brought food, and I was afraid not to eat, lest this might make her return to her idea of my being an *afrit*.

The tin plates were clean and were placed beside us on the floor, where I sat. It was difficult to see what was served out of the cauldrons carried in by two maidservants. The food was dished up in tin cups and looked like chopped straw, though soft, and it contained fat thick pieces of meat resembling eels.

My thoughts went back to the old days at home when we used to catch those squirming 'snake fish,' and to gain time I began to put my hair straight.

"Is this a delicacy of your hills?" I asked pointing to the food.

She gave a laugh. It sounded like a frog's croak.

"We of this clan have eaten naught else. These are rare fishes brought from Hindustan. We keep them and have many in a well in the courtyard. This is a barren land."

I had to manœuvre carefully.

"Yes, it is a strange land. In our hills we do not eat fish, as it is against our religion."

"Then will you partake of bread and of cheese made by our servants from the finest goat's milk?"

"Yes." Anything to escape those fatty pieces lying so near!

The old woman finished her meal and took up a tin bowl of milk, calling the while softly. She now reached behind her bed and brought a snake up on to the clothes, putting the bowl beside it. Its coils unwound slowly. It raised its head and finally put its mouth into the milk.

"This," said the woman, "is one of the Hindustan fishes I saved from the pot."

I became so disgusted that rising I thanked her for her gracious hospitality. Footsteps were heard; quickly the woman put the snake down again as the door opened. A man entered, and I drew down my *yashmak*.

"You have visitors, O pearl of great perfection!"

"Even so, O most perfect warrior!"

Keeping my eyes averted I found myself continually looking for the snake to reappear.

The man inquired for the health of the wife—as I took her to be—and left the room.

"My husband is a great warrior, but gave up fighting when we came here, on account of my beauty. He greatly fears I may be taken by robbers."

She wore a great deal of magnificent jewellery, no doubt the plunder taken from many a caravan. She did not seem to realize the value of it and wore it, she said, only because her husband liked it. She now threw back some of the bedclothes, revealing a beautiful shawl. When I admired it she said her husband had been given it by a friend he had met many years ago passing into Hindustan. I could imagine the poor merchant whose caravan had been surrounded, and the manner of the 'giving.'

"Peace be upon you!" I said. "We have far to go."

"Peace upon you, O stranger! May the spirits guide you safely."

Replacing my *burka*, which I shook thoroughly first, I left the room. There was no servant in view. I was anxious to get away as soon as possible and followed the passage leading down the stairs. At the foot the old woman's husband was standing.

"Peace be upon you, fair one! Will you come this way through the women's quarters that I may talk with you?"

"I am in haste," I replied, "and will speak here."

"In this room, then," and he pushed open the door of a room empty save for the seemingly inexhaustible bundles of clothes.

"I would take under me another wife," he began, while the room seemed to swim round. "Just as you. You would be head of the household and have as much jewellery as you cared to choose from my store. Jewels bright as your eyes, I guess."

"I am already married and require no jewellery, and am in haste."

"Haste, pearl of great value, is not a word we use in these hills."

Through the mesh of the eyelets in my *burka* I looked sideways at him. He must have been well over six feet tall, with a grey beard and the deeply tanned face of an outdoor man. His eyes were

An Isolated Fort in the Hill Country

narrow and close together. His clothes were unlike the heaps lying about, being richly embroidered; his peg-topped trousers were spotlessly white, and a beautiful shawl, folded, hung over his left shoulder. He wore sandals and a white turban. I marvelled how he could keep so clean in such a place. Two hours had passed, and I wondered how my guard was faring. He was all I had to depend upon and I felt glad to have brought him, for it was very unlikely I could ever have reached the place alone.

The robber chief was now at the door.

"Haste not, delight of the world! Make your answer this evening—meantime rest a while. Lest you should require anything there will be a servant outside your door. Your commands are as jewels set in fine gold. I shall return for your answer." Touching his forehead he bowed deeply and closed the door.

What if I could not escape? Suppose I became so hungry as to be forced to eat their food? The window was about two feet square and looked on to the hills. With difficulty I opened it, as quietly as possible lest the servant outside the door should hear anything. The distance to the ground looked to be about fifteen feet, a not inconsiderable depth when one is wearing a *burka*. I thought of the pile of clothes in the room. Was it possible to make these, knotted in strips, into a rope, tie it to the window, climb down, and find the guard and horses? Had the guard been made a prisoner too? No sound reached me from outside to tell me whether anyone was stationed near the door. My jumbled thoughts sorted themselves out. I must escape, for it mattered little in a place like this what my answer was to the brigand chief. My guard disposed of, who but Selima Begum knew where I had gone?

Some of the clothes were so old that they were falling to pieces. By a bit of luck there was a *burka* in the bundles, composed of many yards of a rough, thick material almost like unbleached linen. I tore it into jagged, uneven strips, holding it under other garments to deaden the sound of tearing.

When four strips were torn I knotted them together, hoping that they would hold. There was luckily an iron ring, to which I fastened one end of the improvised rope and threw the rest out of the window. It did not quite reach the ground. I climbed up and having tucked my shoes into my *shulwar* (trousers) I slid down. The knots nearly upset me, and the distance was greater than it looked from the window. With an undignified plump I reached the ground, put on my shoes, and as quick as thought I slipped round the wall, keeping well into the shadow. All was quiet as I approached the front of the house. My guard lay full length on the ground and with relief I saw he was only asleep. Snatching up a stick, I prodded him into wakefulness.

"Horses! We must escape!"

He pointed to the outer gate; I slipped across with beating heart and waited. Our greatest asset was the fact of the fort being unguarded. The brigands had fallen upon lazy ways, perhaps owing to their diet of snakes. I was too nervous to look back, fearful of seeing a face at one of the shattered windows.

The horses were at last outside the gate. However afraid Asaf Khan had been before we arrived at the forgotten fort, he looked brave enough now. This gave me courage. We spoke no word; he led the horses and I followed. Down the side of the hill we went, then mounted and rode at as fast a pace as possible. Asaf Khan handed me an ancient revolver. "There are ten shots. Use them if we are followed, your Honour, and go before me. Those men have no ammunition or guns, but it will only be by the grace of Allah if we escape. May the Holy Pir forgive me for the food I have eaten to-day!"

We saw no more signs of the strange one-time warrior and reached our fort by nightfall. Asaf Khan was overcome by the effects of his meal, and complaining of fatigue I went to bed, to lie awake for hours wondering and wondering again whether my eyes had deceived me. If I doubted that, it was only until the next time I ordered the guard to be ready to accompany me to another fort. "Your Honour," he said, "another experience like the last will not see us alive in this world!"

I dared not tell what we had seen. Asaf Khan was too afraid to mention it, partly no doubt from fear of evil spirits and partly from dislike of being made sport of by his unbelieving friends.

Next time we were told the story of the Snake Valley, Halima Begum said, "Like my respected sister I only believe in what I see," and the 'respected sister' replied:

"Sometimes one can't believe even in that!"

CHAPTER XI

MATCH-MAKING

"I GREATLY miss my sister now she is married and I feel lonely here," said Halima Begum on one of my visits to her home. "My father would have me married to the son of the Chief of Landi but I have seen the young man and care not for him. He is neither so brave nor so handsome as Selima's husband nor my brother. Am I so ugly that I must be given to a man who looks like a camel-driver? What do I care that he is rich and will one day be a great landowner with many fat-tailed sheep, goats, and oxen? I shall not marry him!"

I looked at my pretty sister-in-law and thought surely she ought to have no difficulty in finding a handsome husband.

"But if there is no engagement your father will not force you to marry the man? Remember Syed's difficulties and take heart," I comforted her.

"Yes, but Syed is Father's favourite—he cannot do wrong! I am so very sad, Bhabi Jan. In your country love must be so different. You marry whom you like."

"No, it is not different in my country. There are relations who sometimes make plans for us, as my father did for me," I replied.

"Love must be the same, that is all. Perhaps it is wrong to fall in love."

"Have you fallen in love, Halima Jan?"

The unexpectedness of the question turned Halima Begum's face scarlet. She looked quickly round, and putting a finger to her pursed-up lips uttered a faint "S-shhhh."

"Tell me," I asked excitedly.

"Bhabi Jan, you are like my own sister, I must tell you. I know you will keep my secret."

I promised.

"Have you heard of the Chief of Kota?"

"Yes."

"He has a son of my age. When we were children we played together, but when I went into *purdah* of course we met no more, but I try to hope he has not forgotten me. When he comes here with his father I see him. He is so handsome, but because he does not like these raids the clansmen say he is not brave, and my father would never allow our marriage. I know he is brave because once, long ago, he climbed up to the top of a high rock because I dared him to—I was really sick with fear. Another time he threw himself in front of my run-away pony and was dragged along almost to the edge of a cliff. Had it not been for him I would have been killed. Still, the men think that as he is not fond of raids he cannot be a warrior. It will be well for this land when all the men think as he does."

"Some day perhaps they may. Does your father know anything about this?"

"No, I dare not tell him. He has made up his

mind about the Chief of Landi's son and his stupid wealth, and I'm afraid he will speak to the father soon."

"We must do something before this happens, Halima. Let us think out a plan."

"Bhabi Jan, what can we do? I may neither write nor speak to him. How can he know? And perhaps he has forgotten me after all. My heart aches and will break if I must marry the Chief of Landi's son."

"We must find a way out, Halima Jan. Your father would be lonely if you marry and will not want to be left without you. Shall I speak to him?"

"Please, please, no, Bhabi Jan, I am very shy about it, and would be too terrified to say a word of what I feel to my father. I am too sad to go downstairs," she said as I rose to leave; "say I am resting for an hour."

Instead of going downstairs I went straight to the Chief's business-room and tapped at the door. The "*Balay* [Yes]" in reply was short and crisp. I sensed this was the wrong time. Cautiously opening the door I slipped in.

"*A salaan alaikum* [Peace be upon you]," I ventured.

"*Wa alaikum as salaam* [And peace be upon you also]," came the reply. Standing with his back to the door the Chief was looking out of the window, evidently deep in thought.

"May I speak to you?" I said scarcely above a whisper. Reluctantly I crept farther into the room, which had never seemed so uninviting.

"Do you want anything, Begum Jan? I am rather busy and will come downstairs in about half an hour."

This signified my dismissal, but having got so far I had no intention of retreating.

"Halima Begum seems lonely without her sister," I began.

"It is about Halima Begum I am thinking now. I want to marry her to the Chief of Landi's son. A good family, wide lands! Halima Begum will have all she wants and my anxieties will be over. I am old now and want to see my children happy."

"Yes, happiness is a wonderful thing," I replied clutching a straw. "I should not like Halima Jan to be unhappy."

"Why should she be unhappy, child? Is there anything more she would require?"

"I do not know what she thinks, respected one, but I am told that the Chief of Landi's son is not very brave."

He straightened. "What? Who says so? It is not true! Would I be one to marry my daughter to a coward?"

"I am sure not, that is why I spoke."

"That is a dangerous thing to accuse a man of in these hills, my daughter. Such words have stained these hills red."

"I do not accuse him, but having heard he was not very brave I thought I might tell you in confidence."

"It shall be so. Speak!"

"If you allow me, I prefer not to mention any

names, but you have heard of the raid on Landi a few months ago when the Chief was badly wounded. There were people who thought the son ought to have protected his father and been wounded first. You know in my hills such a thing would have been a disgrace. My clansmen perhaps feel things like that more."

The shot hit its mark.

"Certainly not. How can your clansmen be braver or more courageous than ours? I shall require to think this over—perhaps."

Thus encouraged, I said, "In the old days of clan warfare in my country the sons who allowed their fathers to be wounded while they themselves went safe would never have persuaded *my* countrywomen to marry them."

"That is as it should be, my daughter. Your countrywomen and mine think alike. Leave me now, I am—— It is well you came."

"Thank you, respected one."

"I do not want to have a man in the family who might cause people to question the bravery of the clan," he said shortly. "You speak great wisdom, Begum Jan. Say no word to anyone at present."

"I shall not discuss this with anyone," I said as he opened the door for me to pass through.

My heart throbbed with excitement. I wanted to tell Halima Begum, but was too afraid to give her any encouragement lest nothing materialized, and I would have liked to call out the glad news to every one I met.

Days passed and turned into weeks, and no more

was heard of the proposed engagement. Halima lost all her old gaiety and grieved in secret. I felt glad I had not said anything to her. When we met, the Chief did not mention our conversation. Had he forgotten, I wondered?

Unable to stand the suspense any longer I spoke to him on his next visit.

"How is Halima Begum?"

"You must come oftener to see her, Begum Jan. She misses her sister Selima and grieves a great deal."

"I thought she was to be engaged to a chief's son?" I replied, aghast at my boldness.

"Yes," my father-in-law replied. "I have not quite arranged the matter."

"I am so glad." This escaped my lips out of thankfulness before I was aware of it.

"The difficulty is just where to find a suitable young man."

"I am told that the son of the Chief of Kota is brave and handsome."

"Handsome he may be, but as to bravery he may yet have to win his Arab."[1]

"He is young and may not have had the chance," I protested. "In any case he is not spoken of by the women I meet as the Chief of Landi's son is! Halima Begum has heard what they say, and would be disgraced to have such a husband."

I saw the conversation had had its effect. Still no more was said.

"What family has the Chief of Kota, respected one?"

[1] Show his worth.

"One son and, I believe, a daughter."

"I shall visit her one day soon," I said joyfully, seeing a way out at last. "With your permission perhaps to-morrow."

"As you please, Begum Jan. Go well guarded, it is a long way."

I required no other permission. Syed was not pleased at the thought of my going so far, but I had not mentioned anything to him about Halima Begum's unhappiness, and having received her father's permission I felt well equipped.

The next day soon after dawn I rode off between four well-armed mounted guards. We arrived before midday and I was received by the Kota Chief's wife and her daughter. Neither of them had attended either my wedding or Selima Begum's owing to illness on both occasions, and we had not met before. The Kota Begum was a tall handsome woman with golden hair and real sapphire-blue eyes such as one often sees in these hills, and she made me feel at home immediately.

"Welcome to Kota, Begum Jan! Please consider this house your own and every one in it at your service for as long as you care to honour our eyes with the gladness of your presence."

Over dainty cups of green tea, sitting on the low soft Persian-shawl-covered divans, I told them of my home, education, voyage, and journey. They sat quietly listening, until I mentioned that Halima Begum missed her sister and seemed very unhappy. "I am afraid there is something more than loneliness, she seems quite ill."

"This is indeed a grief to hear. May it be our pleasure to help in any way?"

"I thought a change might do her good, but knowing little of the people around"—a white lie!—"I do not know where she might spend perhaps a week or two."

For just the fraction of a second there was a pause. It was one of those moments when by hesitation one is lost.

"I thought that as this fort is so well known and greatly respected, it would be just the place for Halima Begum," I plunged.

While I recovered from my own boldness the Kota Chieftainess came nearer to me. "Bhabi Jan, I greatly respect your clan, and am always at your right hand. My heart is yours—believe this, and once I hoped it might be possible that the heart of our clan and yours should beat as one. Misunderstandings unfortunately arose and there were mutual enemies who were glad to profit by them. True, we have never taken arms against each other, thanks be to Allah, but—greatly to my distress—we are slightly estranged, although we visit occasionally. There is another member of our family who perhaps shares my feelings."

"Naturally, the Chief of Kota," I added.

"Not so, Begum Golabi Jan [Lady as beautiful as a rose]. My son! He and Halima Begum were playmates and he refuses to take a wife from any of the surrounding forts. My husband will not propose a marriage between his house and yours lest it be refused. This he would greatly resent, and

Allah knows too much blood has flowed already on these hills from such causes. But these are personal things. We would hear of your affairs, Begum Jan."

"I am afraid that as I have such a long journey home it will not be possible to stay longer to-day and it will be necessary for me to take leave of you. Perhaps if you are so kind I may spend a few days here—I had no idea the place was so lovely."

"That indeed will bring great delight to our hearts. Do continue to consider this your home and everything in it yours."

"You are very kind, respected Begum; your warm hospitality makes me confident in asking a request before I go."

"Your slightest wish is happiness to the heart. To hear your desire is to obey it."

"Respected one, may I bring Halima Begum with me for company? It is a long lonely journey."

"Begum Jan, I greatly fear your respected father will not give his consent. Do not, I beg of you, cause any more misunderstanding. Our men put the honour of their women after their submission to God. Old as I am, I would fear to cause strife over such a proposal."

"Do not fear, respected one! If I have your permission to come and bring my sister, leave the rest to me."

The Chieftainess looked sorrowfully away into the distant hills when she said good-bye to me. Her daughter came to the door of the fort.

"*A salaan alaikum*," she said in farewell. "My heart feels lighter for your visit. I love my brother and know he loves Halima Begum, but I have been unable to do anything. You perhaps know what it is to have a brother who is dear to you."

"Yes," I replied, "I understand."

"Then perhaps you know my helplessness—I tell you this because I feel you are trying to help us."

She held my hand tightly in hers. "Come soon, Begum Jan. I shall not rest until you are here."

I left the fort reluctantly. During the long uninteresting journey through the hills I began to think of the risks I had taken. Would either or both clans blame me for hatching a plot? Would I, while trying to put matters right for Halima Begum, cause more difficulties? I felt I could not sleep again until something happened. Syed would be angry. Should I tell him? After all, Halima Begum was his sister. Many times during those long miles I relived the raid I had experienced, and went hot and cold. I was running with the hare and hunting with the hounds. Fatal!

Tired as I was, I was glad to find my father-in-law at our fort. Hurriedly washing the travel grime from face and hands I grasped my courage and went to him and Syed. They were talking in our balcony. I told them about my reception and how kind the ladies at the fort had been and how they had inquired after all the members of the family. When all the nice things I could think of had been recounted, I said I had been invited to spend a week there as the Chieftainess and her daughter, owing to illness, had missed the weddings. The smiles died away. Both my husband and his father evidently thought alike! What would they say when I mentioned Halima Begum? This was not the right time.

My father-in-law rose to go. "I may allow you to visit these people, my daughter, but that you should stay with them is another matter. I regret you cannot go."

"Certainly not," seconded Syed.

All the anger I felt at that moment would have carried any raiders to victory, but this was a raid with a difference.

"Very well, respected one," I said submissively. "I apologize for causing you displeasure."

After the Chief had gone I wrote to the Kota Chieftainess:

RESPECTED ONE,

Peace be upon you.

I enjoyed my visit to you so much to-day. You very kindly invited me to spend a few days at your fort. It will be a great pleasure for me to do so. Perhaps you would be so kind as to include another of my clanswomen in the invitation (which might be sent back by the messenger who takes this to you) as the journey is so long, and it will give me the opportunity of having some one to talk to on the way.

Peace be upon you and upon your clan!

BEGUM JAN OF KOH FORT

How many times the next afternoon did I run to the balcony to catch the first glimpse of the returning horseman! Even a pair of binoculars failed to produce him from those silent hills. At last when I had given up hope of his return I heard horse's hooves clatter into the courtyard. One of my maids was on duty there to receive the reply and in a few minutes I was tearing it open. It ran:

RESPECTED BEGUM JAN,

Your kind visit to us was a great pleasure to my daughter and myself, and we beg of you to excuse us for not having preparations made for your reception, but we hope you will give us another chance of showing you the hospitality we long to extend to you by spending a few days with us here. As it is a long way please give us greater pleasure by bringing one of your kinswomen. We await you with the greatest pleasure, and place ourselves at your feet.

BEGUM SYRA OF KOTA FORT

The next step was to be the worst, to get permission from the Chieftain and my husband to go! The latter I did not fear; with the permission of the former I would not care if Syed refused a dozen times.

The next morning I wrote to the daughter at Kota Fort, fearful lest other plans might develop before my difficulties were solved.

BEGUM ZANUB JAN,

Peace be upon you! Please thank your mother for her kind invitation, which I have the greatest pleasure in accepting. The day after to-morrow I and probably my sister Halima Begum hope to arrive at your fort at about midday. Will you please confide a little in your brother? You know what to say. There is a proverb in my country which says, "A little encouragement goes a long way."

With best wishes,

BEGUM JAN OF KOH FORT

Now to get round the Chieftain!

Summoning the guards I rode to his fort. Luckily my mother-in-law was away visiting, and only Halima and her father were at home. She and I talked a little while, then as if suddenly remembering the invitation I held it out to her.

"Bobo Jan, however have we received this? Has my father relented? It is surely a dream!"

"I must show this to Father and get his permission. I should like very much to go to the Kota Fort," I replied.

"Did you not think his mother lovely—and his sister?"

I noticed the 'his,' but pretended not to. Halima Begum regained some of her old liveliness and began to walk up and down the room.

"Did . . . did you hear of any other members of the clan?"

"The Chieftainess said her son was a great cause of worry to them as he would not marry any of the chieftains' daughters they wanted him to marry."

I turned quickly away, but not before Halima Begum blushed and bit her lower lip to hide her confusion.

"His sister Zanub Begum told me he loves somebody, so we shall probably have a wedding to attend soon," I said walking out on the balcony.

With a spring Halima was beside me.

"Tell me, Bobo Jan, I must know! I am so helpless! I shall die! What is her name?"

I wanted to tease her, but could not bear to look at her agonized face.

"Her name is Halima!"

She laughed and cried at the same time. Then solemnly she said: "What does it matter how much we love each other? My father will never agree to it, even to our visit to Kota Fort. As you know, we may not meet young men, except relatives, after we go into *purdah*. He and I may never meet again."

"That reminds me," I interrupted, "I want to ask Father about ammunition. Later I shall have tea with you before I return to our fort. Please have some of that nice pink tea for me and some of those little ground-almond cakes with the nobbly sugar on them!"

I expected to need some refreshment by that time!

I retrieved the invitation and found the Chieftain reading. I sensed he was in a pleasant mood and we talked of everything for nearly half an hour. It required some courage, more than I seemed to have just then, to approach the subject. My old Nannie's words came back to me as I sat looking across the hills: "There are more ways of getting to the top of the hill than by going straight up."

I would go round this problem too!

"These are beautiful hills—what a pity there is so much strife, respected one!"

"There is not always strife, my daughter."

"It would be a wonderful land if there were none."

"Yes, we do not seek quarrels, but we must defend ourselves and assist our friends."

"It is better for a clan to have many friends, then?"

"Certainly, the more friends the heavier the losses to the enemy."

"It must be a great benefit to make as many friends as possible."

"Yes, so long as one makes honourable friends--that is an important thing."

"Every one must think alike on that point, respected one."

"Not always, I fear. Rather lose one's all to an honourable foe than join forces with a dishonoured clan."

"Has the Kota clan disgraced itself?"

"No, the Chief of Kota and I were boys together. He is brave and fearless. It is a pity we misunderstood each other."

"But I thought you said you were not friendly with the Kota clan. It seems a pity, as the other clanswomen speak highly of them, and they seem very hospitable and courageous. If it is only a misunderstanding perhaps the old friendship may be revived."

The old Chieftain adjusted his glasses. "My family is proud and will not be the first to give in. This man must come to me."

"He may be afraid that you, being the greater chieftain, would not forgive."

"We were staunch friends once. He has saved my life and he once said I saved his."

"How sad that two such brave chieftains should be unfriendly because of a misunderstanding! I am so sorry, as I wanted to stay at the Kota Fort a little while, and I thought that as an invitation came to-day for me and a kinswoman to keep me company, Halima Begum might come too."

It was out! I dared not look at my father-in-law.

He rose from his chair and walked over to the window. There was for me a touch of my last card on the table. A full minute passed. The Chief returned and sat down beside me again. "Little daughter, I am sorry to disappoint you, but you cannot go to Kota."

"I am afraid you will be very angry when I tell you I have already promised."

"Promised! When? How?"

"The day I went there, they asked me to stay the night. I had not made arrangements for that, but promised to return in a few days' time for a week. I have given my word and must go. The visit might do Halima Begum good, too. She is rather pale-looking. Please say yes."

"I once thought the Chief of Kota's son a suitable match for my daughter Halima Begum. He used to be brave; then all at once stories began to reach me which were not so flattering to his courage. My friend the Chief of Landi told me of this."

"It may not have been true, respected one. How terrible if those stories were only rumours! The Chief of Landi might have wanted a pretty wife for his ugly son who looks like a camel-driver!"

The Chief laughed and laughed again. "You forget nothing of what you hear, my daughter!"

"Of course I could not forget having seen the ugly son of the Landi chief." It was now my turn to laugh.

"Certainly he is not greatly favoured with good looks, but he has wealth and bravery."

"The son of Kota's Chief is handsome and wealthy, respected one. Four different chiefs want him to marry their daughters. That shows he does not lack bravery."

"When a man is brave he shows it, even as age whitens the hair of the head."

"May we go to the Kota Fort, if only for a day? I would not have them say we did not know what a promise meant."

"No, I would not have that, my daughter. Go then to-morrow, spend the night, and return here the following afternoon. Take as many guards as you please."

How simple after all is the warrior's heart! I wanted to hug the old Chieftain, but kissed his hand instead, and asked permission to go to have tea with Halima Begum. Once outside the door I remember nothing of the intervening passages between there and Halima Begum's room. As I opened her door she was sitting with her face in her hands, the picture of despair. Raising her head I saw her eyes were red with weeping.

"We are to go to the Kota Fort for the night to-morrow!"

"Do not joke with me, Bhabi Jan!"

"I am not joking, your father has just given permission." We danced round the room, then over the tea-cups spoke of my talk to her father.

"I would never have dared as you did, Bhabi

Jan. How can I thank you? Tell me anything I can do for you?"

"Marry the man who is waiting for you, that's what I want!"

"How happily would I respect your wishes if it were possible."

"It *is* possible. Now pack and I shall go home and do the same."

Syed scarcely believed me, but was quite willing for me to go.

"Why does not Father marry Halima to the Kota Chief's son?" I asked him as I packed my clothes.

"You see, there is some misunderstanding between our father and his. The young fellow somehow gets the name of 'glass-heart'[1] and you know what effect that would have on Father. He specializes in warriors for his daughters!"

"Not always handsome ones, if the Landi youth is his choice."

"No, he's not much to look at, but that's not everything."

"It is considerable if one has to live with it, though."

"I wish the old boys would make it up all the same, *bul-bul*.[2] They've given this boy a bad name, and that is difficult to live down in these parts. He must do something worthy of notice before the brand is forgotten."

"That should not be difficult here," I replied.

Next morning with greatly subdued excitement we started for the Kota Fort. The Chieftainess and

[1] Coward. [2] Nightingale.

her daughter had certainly spent all the time having the fort decorated for our reception, and received us as though we had been two returned prodigals! The night of our arrival we had a great feast preceded by wrestling matches in the courtyard. Halima Begum had eyes for only one man there, and it was evident by his many successes and the ringing cheers rising from his followers that the 'little encouragement' had had the desired effect.

"I have spoken to my brother," Zanub Begum whispered at the first opportunity. "The men say he is his old self again."

In the midst of another wrestling competition that followed the feast at an hour nearing midnight, the guards opened the gates to a caravan seeking shelter for the night. The men of the caravan had been on the road to Peshawar with *khultas* of dried fruit and carpets when they were attacked by about fifty men. They recognized the leader as a notorious brigand. The unexpectedness of the attack when they were almost out of the danger area had taken them by surprise, and when they showed fight they were savagely treated and all their wares were taken by the robbers. One old man had had his right hand completely severed because he offered to fight any brigand single-handed rather than give up his fruit.

The Kota clansmen were so infuriated that they agreed to go back after the band of brigands and retrieve the goods. It took but a few minutes for the wrestlers to don their coats, put on their cartridge-belts, and arm themselves for the fray.

The courtyard was soon like the preparation for a battle.

"Look, there he is!" said Halima Begum, gripping my arm. Below in the courtyard was a seething mass to me, but Halima Begum was in love—for her there was only one man in that jostling crowd.

It was the next night when the Kota men came home. Many had been wounded, some were dead—I knew what Halima Begum was thinking as those improvised stretchers were carried across the courtyard.

Again and again I wondered whether this was the end of the romance. I would not allow Halima Begum to join the Chieftainess and her daughter when they went down to the room where the wounded lay. Her hands were as cold as ice, but she betrayed no emotion. She was too overcome by the tragedy to speak.

Presently Zanub Begum came rushing to the balcony. "My brother! My brother is safe! Thanks be to Allah!" The spell was broken. Halima Begum seemed too stupefied to grasp the significance of the words for some minutes. Then putting both arms round my neck she wept.

It was midnight when we had our evening meal, which none of us seemed to have missed until we saw the food! Afterwards the clansmen gathered in the courtyard and an elder of the village called for silence.

"I would speak to you all, O men of the Kota clan, so that those of you who did not accompany us and those of you too young to be with us may yet hear of bravery. See yonder on the hill-tops the blaze of bonfires! Those are lit to the honour of the men of Kota who captured the outlaw and his brigand band—the brigand who has terrorized these hills for four years and who was caught to-day in one of the bravest attacks the men of Kota Fort have ever made. It was long ere we sighted the brigands travelling together with three merchandise-loaded camels stolen from the travellers —who are our guests until such time as they are able to continue their journey. It was long again ere we got near them, creeping behind the boulders and on the lower side of the hills, which as you all know is the difficult part. Suddenly we opened fire. Like the flash of a *tulwar* they turned and were upon us, rolling boulders down the hill. By the beard of the Holy Pir, it was as though the furies were upon us. By the blessings of Allah we kept our heads, though many of our men must have lost their rifles. Soon we came to grips with the brigands, and, by Allah, huge they were and without mercy. Again and again we were beaten back and were near to defeat, for our numbers were becoming less, when our Chief's son, Hafiz Khan—all honour to him!—who had fought from the first with his *tulwar*, and now was the only man with a gun, put a number of the brigands out of the battle and called again and again to the men of Kota to rally.

"The chief brigand was behind a boulder above us.

" 'Cowards,' called he, 'whoever you are, you call yourselves warriors when there are forty to one!'

" 'We are no cowards, son of a jackal,' called the Chief's son, and to show you I myself will fight with you even to death. Stand back, men of Kota, that this man may swallow his lie in the presence of you all. Come from your hiding-place, son of wickedness.'

"The brigand came forward. Slowly the two men approached each other, the brigand being fully four inches taller than the son of our Chief. Suddenly they leaped at each other. The air was slashed as each man sprang from the blade-thrust of the other. The robbers returned at a safe distance to watch the spectacle of a youth who dared to face alone the terror of the hills. It was a sight you should all have witnessed."

The hills now echoed with the applause—away across the village the bonfires jagged the darkness. Round after round of cheering rent the air. The men grew hoarse; all called the name of Hafiz Khan, the hero of the raid. The narrator raised a silencing hand.

"Long they fought, my brothers. Both were wounded, and at last the brigand turned the knife on himself with these words: 'No longer am I fit to lead you, my brave ones, when a youth such as you see for yourselves can wound my sword-arm.' "

All was excitement. Every one ran to congratulate the hero of the hour, who had sought refuge in his room. A maid brought a letter to Halima Begum, which she read and then handed to me. It ran:

> All I have done this night I have done for you, Gulabi Dil [Rose Heart]. Always your face has been before me. This heart and hand are yours while life lasts.
> HAFIZ KHAN

Thus Hafiz Khan won his bride.

CHAPTER XII

AHMED THE BOLD AND SILENT

I HAD called Ahmed, one of my servants, thrice; the third time the owner of the name appeared beside me in the rose-garden, while I noticed, but pretended not to, the figure of a veiled woman slide along the wall to the servants' quarters some hundred yards away.

"Bring my sherbet at once." I fancy he followed my eyes, and, looking slightly embarrassed, hurried away for the drink.

Up till then there had been no woman in the life of my slow, faithful servant. As a matter of fact, lack of looks and money present their own difficulties, for a man, even though a servant, must be able to give a dowry and jewellery of some kind to his bride. Ahmed was, to boot, slightly simple, although he said his prayers five times a day as regularly as any *mullah*. He was not simple enough to take the wrong change, or to be lingering without occupation when the tall Pathan moneylender replete with stick called for any belated instalments on his loan. His carelessness and almost characteristic dress were the chief peculiarities denoting the not quite complete grasp of essentials. Dress he treated like the worldly thing it is. It had little place in his life. Again and again I gave him white trousers, dark blue coat, and blue and white turban like the rest of the menservants. Repeatedly I added the same advice as to their preservation, but always within the week the clothes he wore might have been taken from a ragbag. Just exactly what he did to give them that look of streaky griminess remained a mystery. Once I talked to him seriously, threatening dismissal, because he appeared before me in an old dressing-gown which my husband had worn longer than he would care for me to make public, yet the look half tolerant, half simple, never left Ahmed's face.

"Sherbet, your Honour." My train of thought was interrupted by the return of the untidy one.

"Who were you speaking to near the kitchen a few minutes ago?" I asked in the way people do when they intend to be answered truthfully.

Ahmed appeared to have discovered something wrong with his shoes, so persistently did he fix his gaze upon them. He evidently had difficulty in making use of his tongue. The smile broadened, then narrowed, in a conscious effort to present the immobile features demanded of a good servant. Still no reply. The silence was sufficient reply for me, or for anyone else who can read symptoms.

"All right. Go." He had committed himself, and I needed time to think, for the lady of his choice, if my eyes did not deceive me, was at least twenty years his senior, the mother of two particularly noisy and difficult sons; and as to beauty, the only claim she had was the illusion her veil gave, for Time had these many years made a race-track of her face.

Muntaz was a maid to Halima Begum, and I had had the opportunity poor Ahmed would not have until too late for remedy, of seeing her as she really was. Being a Muslim she was always carefully veiled, except to the women and master of the household. To the rest Muntaz drew her veil—and drew it remarkably coquettishly for her age. Moreover, it was generally a pink veil, delicate rose, and profusely scented. Now this ought to have attracted even a man with the full percentage of wits, but since the demise of the first husband it unfortunately never had.

I was not particularly anxious for Ahmed to start his own *ménage*, for, being the only servant whose troubles were those of a bachelor, he was always free and willing to be on duty the whole day. Alas, now that Cupid had built a nest in his heart, I would be the loser!

Ahmed was not handsome; even his blue and white turban, which he tied smartly, could not make him prepossessing. The beard too, which he affected although he was only about twenty years of age, was not cultivated in any hope of adding manliness or importance to his person, but rather to save a few precious minutes in the morning for one who slept heavily and started a new day unwillingly. He always slept within call, and I am confident that, on the few occasions I summoned him to investigate strange noises during the night, he had not had sufficient time to dress and get from his balcony, although he appeared just as he was when he was dismissed until wanted.

Romance never buds and seldom blossoms where we can see it. I began to fear lest the simpleton in love might find when it was too late that he had married some one old enough to be his mother. My thoughts were rudely disturbed by sudden yells coming from the direction of the servants' quarters.

Muntaz, passing at the time, carefully veiled as usual, told me, in answer to my question as to the explanation of so unseemly a noise, that it would be Ahmed chastising her sons. The idea of the mild Ahmed having even an idea which led him to use force amused me. I appeared surprised and asked how it came about that my servant should spend my time looking after her boys. She replied with shyness which would have enhanced the youthful charm of a girl thirty years her junior that "Ahmed helps me with them."

This but confirmed my worth as a psychologist. Whatever Muntaz must have been in the days of her youth I cannot say, but although youth failed her now coquetting did not. She was even coy with me.

I began to look for the usual signs of the enamoured man in the dress of my servant, but so far as that was concerned things remained as usual. Evidently Ahmed had decided that if romance was to blossom it would not be on account of his smart clothes.

One night after the evening meal when green tea was being placed in little pink tumblers on the balcony, I caught sight of Ahmed picking roses, all the while smiling out in the evening air. This I took as the last straw, for the servant was not the type to toy with scented blossoms, so, calling him, I asked, "Why are you taking so much interest in Muntaz's children?"

It was even as I feared. Worse, for from time to time he sniffed at the rose petals in his hand. There was no necessity for him to reply. He stood uneasily first on one foot, then on the other, pushed his turban agitatedly down on his brow, and smiled in a soft way.

Now Eastern people take interest in all the affairs of their servants, who in turn bring any difficulties to their master. The master's word is final, and they obey it like children, never making any remark except in agreement.

The interview had ended. The next thing was to approach Muntaz. She came at once on knowing I wanted her, well veiled. I felt grateful to that veil, as she too might well have been, as it was her best friend.

Although continuing with the usual coquetting, she admitted that Ahmed wanted to marry her.

"But he cannot give you a dowry."

"He has an uncle who may do that," she replied.

"An uncle! But has this uncle no daughter of his own that he should provide a dowry for his nephew's wife?"

"I know not, your Honour, but by what Ahmed said we are depending on that."

"He is very young to take the responsibility of your family."

"He manages them very well, your Honour. The children are fond of him. I was very young when I married." There might have been another opinion about that.

"Oh," I said with surprise. A veil hides the face only, not the many common little habits which betoken the stress such moments impose—the agitation of unoccupied hands—the adjustment of a veil not requiring any attention—the slight sniff, better than nothing during a difficult silence.

"Are you willing to marry him?"

"If your Honour will allow me."

The answer took me by surprise. Soft answers do avert wrath, and once my wrath is turned I weaken and become apologetic. Here I did not weaken, at least not too much. What I did do was to reply that having no idea such a thing was being contemplated I would think it over—knowing full well that when two people want to marry, opposition only hurries on the ceremony. Any resistance is like drawing a picture on the water.

For a few days I did think it over, during which time I delicately when in a good humour and indelicately when not pointed out to my servant the responsibilities of providing for some one else's children, and the rather mixed blessing of marrying somebody much older than himself. Also, I continued, "what dowry can you give her?"

"That, your Honour, may require a slight arrangement."

"Good," thought I, feeling more secure in my position.

"My uncle, a cook to a neighbouring chief, may with some conversation on the subject aid me."

"And how do you propose to approach him?"

"Well, your Honour, he is greatly attached to me and has saved money."

"How can he save money when he has so many daughters."

"Allah knows, your Honour! I shall, with your permission, visit him one day and ask many questions!"

"Will he not wonder why you should want to marry a woman older than your mother, with two children."

"All these wonderments are quite possible, for my uncle is a man of much inquisitiveness."

For a time I had thought it possible to make him see my point of view, but finally the last straw was swept away. There was only one way out of this, the sacrifice of my servant. I could not see how he could run her affairs and yet have time for mine.

"Does this mean you are leaving my service? You are the fourth generation of your family to serve the Chiefs."

"Not so, your Honour. Rather than leave the service I will place my own wishes after yours."

The thought of these two moping round the place made the decision, and next day after the evening meal Ahmed presented himself.

"My uncle will give the money and promises to let me know the amount within a week."

A week later the money was forthcoming—fifteen tomans (about £15)—and the ceremony was to take place at once. This being the servants' treat, we gave the feast money and allowed them to invite some neighbouring servants. Muntaz was elated and the pink veils she began to exhibit proved but a beginning. My gifts to her were sandals, a *burka*, some long shirts and trousers for the wedding; everybody gave her something.

Ahmed, on the other hand, did not even change his much-discussed trousers, torn as they were. The old blue and white turban, the end of which had been no doubt used surreptitiously a few times to give the final polish requisite before my cup would pass muster, remained, and he continued to wear a sheepish look. Having put on the blue coat seemed enough effort in wedding preparation for this wooer, who had without doubt won on the sheer strength of his personality!

The wedding-day arrived. The ceremony performed in my little workroom was over. There but remained the formality of 'unveiling the bride.' Only employers and near relatives witness this—which, if she be beautiful, must be *the* moment.

Muntaz retired, as is the custom, to a small room adjoining, where she sat on the floor in front of two fellow-servants holding a looking-glass. I got as near as possible to see the surprise on the face of Ahmed when he would raise the veil. He approached through the doorway and when he reached the bride looked over her shoulder ready to raise the veil and see her reflection in the glass.

We were all agog with excitement. We knew the looks of Muntaz, but wondered what effect looks *plus* obvious age would have on the bridegroom. He moved the veil and revealed the most artful of reddened cheeks and lips and the kohl-laden eyes. We were disappointed in the lack of impression portrayed on the features of Ahmed, the new husband. I began to think his simplicity a pose to hide the strength of the man within.

After the evening meal the only visible sign of celebration Ahmed showed as he carried in the coffee was a garland of roses round his neck; another garland he deposited on the left side of my coffee-cup. That was his celebration.

Had he noticed the *passé* beauty of his wife he did not advertise it. The same semi-permanent smile played over his face. The same untidy dress adorned his person.

Time passed—it became the order of the day to hear shrill screams interrupted by what sounded like the welts of an accurately placed shoe. Ahmed evidently had the situation well in hand.

Still he continued in the old way; the slight simplicity remained. One could not help admiring the courage with which he tackled the family he had married! His service never faltered, even when he was obliged to put down a tray in order to administer a shoe-beating. Beauty has perhaps not the same place in everybody's life after all.

CHAPTER XIII

COMEDY OF A LITTLE KING

AN invitation came for us to spend a few months with a rajah in India. We had met him on several occasions previously and had corresponded with him since. He wrote that he had invited a large party for Christmas celebrations and intended to go into camp for the shooting. He was very anxious to entertain us and hoped we would not refuse the invitation.

I approached my father-in-law, who promised to think it over. A day later he came to visit us and said he did not consider we ought to accept, as India was a long and not very safe journey from our hills, and the Rajah was a Hindu and worshipped idols, holding cows sacred and building temples to monkey-gods. He did not approve of idolatry or of men who wore jewellery and were reputed to be not very particular about how their relatives disappeared if there was any fear of their becoming too powerful. People who used poisons, he maintained, were as snakes in the grass, and as such were better avoided.

"I should like to see India, having heard so much of it on our voyage."

"It is not always wise to be inquisitive, my daughter, but if you have set your mind on this journey, I do not want to be between you and the sun.[1] When does this idol-worshipper ask you to be present?"

"We are invited in a month, respected Father."

"Does my son approve of this visit?"

"He says if I care to go he too will go."

"You must come of a clan without fear. Your countrymen must be brave when young people of your age contemplate such dangers so quietly."

"What dangers?"

"You have been in danger ever since your arrival, my daughter, and I have been greatly troubled by your desires to wander outside the fort. I fear no more for the future of this clan, but would beg of you to restrict your wanderings. You are ignorant of these hills."

"I promise, and am pleased to have your permission to go to India, respected one."

"Return quickly, then. I shall miss you and the little one, and have great anxiety as to your safety among idol-worshippers," and patting my head he walked slowly away.

Permission being obtained, we prepared to get our things ready. It was a great disappointment to me to find it was not safe to take much jewellery with me through the Khyber. Nevertheless I managed to tuck some away in unexpected places and hoped for the best, as our caravan was to be well guarded.

On the day of our departure the relations came to see us off. They did not approve of our visit to

[1] Stand in your way.

the Indian prince and a few of the women secretly gave me charms to ward off all kinds of evil which in their opinion would be our daily lot in far-away Hindustan.

A strong armed party of the clansmen was to take us to the borders of the '*ferungi* land.' My father-in-law gave us many gifts for the Rajah, though I have no doubt he penanced himself with prayers for doing so. The gifts included Persian lambskin coats, gold slippers, turquoise jewellery and rugs, fat-tailed sheep, dried mulberries, apricots and walnuts.

"Become not an idol-worshipper, my sister, whatever they offer you," said Selima Begum solemnly.

"The wrath of God is upon these Hindus," said a pious *mullah* who came to give us his blessing.

"Be persuaded while you are amongst friends," begged my mother-in-law.

So with the united blessings of the clan we left for Hindustan.

"Peace be upon you!"

"Allah protect you!"

"Our blessings wherever you are!" they called after us as they sadly watched our departure.

A servant ran to say that the Chieftain "would watch the hills with weary eyes for our return." The dear old man was not the tyrant he wanted us to believe and would have come with us had we required him, idols or no.

Our caravan was well guarded and the journey though long was without incident. The robbers of the hills evidently thought us too well protected; other travellers joined us and our caravan must have been miles long. At Peshawar we took farewell of our guards, who watched us until we disappeared from sight. I expect to their ideas our journey must have appeared a mild attack of madness, for they knew nothing and cared less about any land except their own. As we passed through the 'turnstile' into British India I felt more sad to leave the hospitality of the 'Free Land' behind me than I had been afraid to enter from the last post of British territory on that nerve-shaking journey over two years ago.

The bustle of Peshawar after the long spell of hill quietness seemed futile. Everybody looked disturbed and anxious. They differed greatly from the clansmen, who seemed able to tackle any situation with a calmness foreign to these short, dark-skinned shopkeepers. From Peshawar we took train to Delhi. The journey down to the capital was quite pleasant owing to its being the cool season. The climate from September until February is like a lovely Western summer. At every station fruit- and sweet-sellers, cool drinks, and watermen appeared. The journey was like one long picnic. For one rupee it was possible to buy a basket of lovecots (delicious yellow plums), plantains, bananas, melons, and fried monkey-nuts. The servants, Ahmed and Muntaz, who had begged to go to the '*ferungi* land' with us, were delighted as children. Margaret's *ayah* (nurse) also refused to leave us. Ahmed and Muntaz travelled in the servants' carriage, while the nurse and child were in the carriage next to us along the corridor.

We passed miles upon miles of sugar-cane, which looked neglected and appeared to belong to nobody; then miles of barren land, though fertile-looking compared to the 'Free Land' hills. The people themselves were quite a different type, dark, short, and looked as though they were perpetually bullied. Their talk sounded strange after Pushtu. They spoke more quickly, gesticulated greatly with their hands, but were otherwise lethargic. At the station there seemed no proper time-table; so many times the guard had to speak to the engine-driver that he might have been telling instalments of a long story. Eventually we arrived at Dumpur. Royal cars and chauffeurs met us, and, with a number of other guests who arrived at the same time, we were driven to the guest-house. This was near the Palace and staffed with many servants. Guests who had not brought their own servants were waited upon by these retainers, who looked very different from our hill-men, and barely half the size, but were very anxious to please us. They lacked the independence of the tall hill-men.

The guest-house was a splendid building, beautifully furnished, surrounded by lovely gardens. Six Royal cars were placed at the disposal of guests, who could drive where they liked. After a rest we went to the Palace to call upon his Highness the Rajah.

That night, December 21, there was to be a great fancy-dress ball at the Palace. We were asked if we had brought fancy dresses, and, if not, we were requested to make use of the State *durzis* (dressmakers), men who could work quickly and efficiently and follow any design, however rudely sketched, without any tiresome 'trying on,' completing a fancy dress at the cost of a few shillings. With only a few hours to spare the idea seemed impossible, but almost by magic these men arrived with sewing-machines and small boys loaded with every material produced in Manchester and the State bazaar. Some hours later I was successfully turned out as the new moon, in draperies of midnight blue, star-spangled, with a silver crescent moon on my forehead.

We assembled in the great reception-hall, where the Ranee and Princesses greeted us. Being Hindus they wore no veils. The Ranee was young and lovely, which fact, it was freely said, weighed more in the opinion of the Rajah than pedigree.

The guests trooped in—Indian ladies in gorgeous *saris* and lovely jewels; rulers of other states; Western women and their husbands, who in their plain black clothes with white shirt-fronts looked like magpies hopping about among the sunbeams.

His Highness received us in true Indian fashion, making us all welcome and at ease. Being on my first visit to an Indian State, I was greatly excited and perhaps a trifle too optimistic. After a few minutes' chat, we were taken to the banqueting-hall. My place being on the Rajah's left and directly opposite the other members of his family, I had a good opprotunity of enlightenment at first-hand.

There were perhaps two hundred guests, the women vying with each other as to whose 'creation' was the 'last word' from 'home'—in a polite way, of course, and done in the best manner. My partner was a hill-chieftain of huge proportions, arrayed in a flauntingly tied turban. The jewellery of the Englishwomen paled to insignificance before that of the princes of the many states represented, who gazed admiringly or condescendingly, no doubt, as the jewellery warranted, at each other.

Wine flowed into the glasses—such champagne as one could but expect at a prince's table. The few Muslims present respected their religion and took only water. The majority of other faiths, however, did more than justice to his Highness's cellar. Some knew their capacity and, I imagine, had the fun of the proverbial onlooker. Half-way through the long meal it was evident that a number of my neighbours intended to make something of a red-letter night of it.

Ice-cream was being served, and very welcome it was, for the heat and the cigar and cigarette smoke began to make us feel slightly uncomfortable. The Rajah by this time was feeling the sultry heat so much that, casting discretion to the winds, he had removed his curled wig—necessary for his 'period' dress—and placed it, curls down, in his ice-cream.

"Damned hot," he exclaimed, to which everybody agreed. They had reached the stage when they did agree to everything, as though it had been their own exclusive thought.

"This is hot, too," he went on, retrieving the pink ices from under the wig, which he set again on his head, well to the back—from where the melted ice dripped down somewhere behind.

When the fun had reached its height and we had all become infectiously gay, some one proposed that my small daughter should be fetched. Now Margaret was only four and a half years old and had been in bed since six o'clock. It was now eleven o'clock, but before I could expostulate I heard the order given for the child to be brought at once. I felt as any other mother would in similar circumstances. I expected that Margaret would be terrified at the unaccustomed scene and would probably cry loudly and incessantly.

But it would have been useless for me to protest. The company was now in a mood to insist on this new source of entertainment, and thrice footmen were sent to find out the cause of delay. To begin with, it took an hour to go to the guest-house and back again, and the child had to be dressed and make the return journey in the car.

The remainder of the banquet was not much enjoyment to me, but no one, I consoled myself, would have guessed. After an hour and a half, while we were toying almost revoltingly with chocolates and crystallized fruits, the vision appeared at the door—Margaret in her pink frilly party frock carried by a footman with three others bringing up the rear. She was too overcome to say anything, and scarcely recognized her mother in the 'new moon' dress. The Rajah placed her on his knees, and she at once engaged herself with ice-cream and maraschino cherries. Only once did she look at me—turning in all the triumph which even grown-ups feel for things forbidden. The State National Anthem struck up; his Highness, much to my relief, grew tired of his plaything, and the procession of footmen bearing a small flushed child out of the banqueting-hall was a welcome sight to me.

The Rajah had now reached the door, followed by the guests, who were all looking forward to the cool air after the suffocating heat of the room. The highly polished floor did not assist the steps of some members of the company; and when they had with difficulty negotiated their way to the exit they seemed incapable of keeping to the paths in spite of the hundreds of Japanese lanterns that dispelled the darkness. My husband, who had drunk nothing stronger than water during the banquet, suddenly found a pair of arms flung round his neck and, overbalanced by the suddenness of the attack, shot forward into the garden. Here the Chief Minister was already in difficulties with his turban, which had fallen to the ground, and, as it is generally those least fitted for such a task who undertake it, there were eight people trying to extricate him and finally themselves from the many yards of golden tissue of which the turban was composed. The sight was one of the most amusing I have ever witnessed, and was evidently unique, for the Minister was heard to say that he had never known his turban behave in this way before!

The guests formed up behind the Rajah and my husband, and we made our way to another room, where nautch girls were to give a display of

Indian dancing. Sofas and easy chairs were plentiful, but all were immediately occupied, for a good many of the guests appeared to have been overcome by the change in temperature complained of by our host.

The dancing 'girls' were not prepossessing and were no longer young. Their men-folk composing the orchestra were still less so—but both were well received. It was now long past midnight, and those of us who had travelled far began to feel the strain. One Englishwoman, the wife of a Government official, proposed to the State doctor that she would like to say good-night to the Rajah and retire. The doctor was greatly agitated at the announcement, and informed those around generally that it was an unheard-of thing for anyone to go before his august master—who was now all but asleep on the most comfortable sofa. At this point a number of the women would have trusted to the sound sleep of his Highness and left the room, but the Ranee and the Princesses were wide awake and carrying off the honours.

Snores now began to be heard from different parts of the room even above the music. While it was scarcely etiquette to arouse the somnolent guests, it was far from polite for these men to snore in the presence of their hostess, and taking courage—all of which was needed—a few of the chief officials took it upon themselves to keep the would-be sleepers aware of the proceedings.

There seemed no end to this *tamasha* (amusement) and 3.30 A.M. found us in various collapsed conditions. Even the *aides-de-camp* were overcome by the added exertions, and the original sleepers remained where they were until getting-up time. In one corner a highwayman's mask had fallen over his nose, and his 'booty' was doing duty as a pillow for a friar. A Russian soldier had taken off his long boots, and his feet, on which some Spanish toreador had hung his coat, were perched on the arm of his sofa.

Still the gesturing of the dancers continued, while the music waxed louder than ever. His Highness now awoke and seemed at last to have had enough of the entertainment. After a few minutes he gave his wig another push, this time well over his brow, while a bald patch showed in shining aloofness at the back. With a "Good night" which included everybody, he got up, and, attended by his staff, made his way to the door amid heartfelt sighs of relief from the weary guests who could hardly keep their eyes open.

We rose and prepared to go to the guest-house for the remnant of the night. Truth to tell, we were beyond caring whether or where we went!

Next day outdoor games started after lunch. We gathered for the grand gymkhana to watch pillow-fighting, wrestling, racing, and shooting. Great consternation reigned when the Rajah found that the wings of the birds had been cut, thus making them useless. It was suggested to his Highness that the culprit must be the Chief Secretary, who wanted to spoil the sport! The truth was that a jealous rival official, always anxious to belittle others (no doubt with a view to a Chief Secretaryship), had cut the wings. His plausibility was second only to that of Uriah Heep, and his jolly outward demeanour and loud laugh formed an effective mask for his cunning ways. The incident spoiled the day for most of us, for everybody knew the truth except the Rajah, but did not want to associate themselves with the telling of it. The Chief Secretary was on duty from 6 A.M., and as he was often summoned to the Palace at all hours of the night when ideas of more than usual importance occurred to his master, it was necessary for him to sleep lightly. Moreover, he was a Muslim and not welcomed by the Hindu employees.

The poor A.D.C.s, of whom there were twenty, seemed to me to stand at attention the whole day in the heat. The only respite given them was when they were, as part of their duty, compelled to play cards with the guests. This they did every night, looking the picture of trembling fear. The stakes were not high, it is true, but neither was their pay, and their anxiety was reflected in the unfortunate results of an evening's games, when they rose from the tables after having lost their next month's wages.

Our host was a keen sportsman and enjoyed hastily arranged shooting-parties. The *shikar* (hunt) was good sport. Both men and women took part, and we set off on elephants, shooting from the howdahs. There was a prize of fifty rupees each day to the person who made the biggest bag. We were given to understand by the Chief Minister, a true diplomat, that of course it was a rule of the State that no one ever shot more than his Highness!

A Fountain under a Grape-vine in the Courtyard of a Pathan's House

The competitions became slightly involved, although we were all saved by the astuteness of one of the State *shikaris*, who collected our game to swell the count of his master. Each night after dinner we assembled with the totals of our respective bags, which, thanks to the *shikari*, never exceeded that of his royal master. Our congratulations, I hope, sounded sincere.

Meanwhile, the Palace was haunted by fat and anxious *bunias* (money-lenders) who had called to see whether they might be lucky enough to receive even a portion of the first instalment of considerable loans they had each made to various persons about the Court years before. They were politely asked to wait. Any further anxiety on their part was met by the same soothing reply, for India is ever a land of "To-morrow." At length, as was to be expected, even these determined gentlemen ceased to have more time to waste in profitless loitering, and, giving up the pursuit, made their way as best they could on foot along the dusty roads to the station.

One money-lender told me that a special messenger had come to him, asking when it would be convenient for him to travel to the State in connexion with an important and pressing matter which would result in considerable profit to him. He hastily obeyed the summons: at the station a luxurious car met him, and after completing a transaction involving a loan of many thousands of rupees he was driven back in the same way. Yet since that day which promised new wealth he had not seen one rupee of the loan; and he was now additionally out of pocket owing to the many journeys he had made to the State in the vain hope that the borrower would remember him. "Many times I coming," he said to me pathetically, "many times I going. No can meeting, no food being giving. Truly am I desolated!"

Owing to the different laws governing each State, no claim can be made by outsiders for repayment of any loan to a State official. Each State is a law unto itself, and no hand can be laid upon anyone owing money anywhere in India so long as the debtor remains in one of these States, where many undesirables shelter and into which many bad debtors disappear.

My servants had too much time on their hands, and being afraid they might employ themselves to their disadvantage, I readily agreed to their request that they might go fishing. Not knowing much about Hinduism, I was excusably unaware of the fact that no fish are allowed to be caught in this particular State. Twice Abdullah, my Indian Muslim servant, brought very fine fish home. The third time he was anxious to have his catch cooked for me and took it to the guest-house *khansama* (cook) to have it prepared as a surprise for my breakfast. The fish was delicious, but the surprise came later when the Secretary told me he had almost lost his job when the knowledge came to the Rajah that my servant had taken a sacred fish from forbidden waters—for the belief is that the spirits of dead relations enter into these fishes and are happy! Certainly, although such is not my belief, I was far from happy when thinking of that breakfast in retrospect.

The Ranee and the Princesses had no hobbies. In these circumstances their interests were centred on clothes and jewellery. They were always beautifully dressed, and although they invariably wore *saris* their shoes were the daintiest the West could provide. Shopkeepers from many large towns sent representatives with selections of everything likely to appeal to the eyes of the State ladies and their guests. The temptation to buy more than one could conveniently afford was considerable; and some of the guests occasionally put too literal a construction on the suggestion that they should "pay any time," with the result that many of the shopkeepers who had some knowledge of English business methods refused to allow credit.

The Rajah gave hundreds of gifts at Christmas, chiefly jewellery, and it was the Secretary's by no means enviable task to arrange for jewellers to bring a selection of their wares. There was a formidable list of his Highness's relatives, friends, and leading officials who were to receive presents, and the perspiring Secretary had worked all night to think out suitable gifts not exceeding the price fixed by the Rajah. The jewellery was to be set out in the strong-room, where the Secretary was to go and choose the presents. Each gift had to be wrapped, the name of the recipient written on the package, and a suitable greeting attached. My husband and I secretly helped the overworked Secretary by packing things the whole of one night; he would never have completed his task otherwise. The messages had still to be written out after he had taken them down in shorthand; this occupied him for another day and night. When all were finished, he reported to his Highness, who was evidently again feeling the difference in temperature acutely! He asked what message had been put on a certain relative's packet. When told it was "With very much love," he said that it was too strongly worded and was merely to read "A happy Christmas." This was the case with nearly a hundred packages, and the Secretary was almost crazy with the repeated alterations. When everything had been gone over for the hundredth time, it was discovered that the alleged thermos flask provided for the Rajah's aunt turned out to be a brooch made of sacred jay's feathers.

We were told one morning at breakfast that there would be shooting the next day, and his Highness would be delighted if we cared to join the party. The Rajah went to one of his houses twelve miles away in his Rolls-Royce, taking with him the *shikaris*, who were to drive back in the horse-drawn brake with the dogs. The Secretary accompanied his master to bear the responsibility of seeing that the dogs and guns were properly loaded into the conveyance, although he had never seen a gun-dog nearer than ten yards.

All went well until the return journey, when the rain came on just as the car reached the Palace. The Rajah blamed the Secretary for not having the dogs' conveyance covered, and was in a panic lest the dogs got wet. The Secretary would have to return along the road until he met them, and the point was stressed that this would be the last time a thing of the kind ought to happen. Back the Secretary had to go on foot, as no car had been ordered from the Palace, and no chauffeur dared take one out without the Royal command. Many miles the man had to walk before coming upon the *shikari* and his dogs—quite dry and safe, in spite of the downpour.

The Secretary by this time was glad to get into the vehicle, where, after three nights' hard work and no sleep, he lay down on the floor and was soon fast asleep. When he awoke he was in the Palace yard, instead of having been deposited at his own bungalow, which he reached on foot after an hour's good walk—only to find an urgent telephone message waiting from the Palace, asking that he should report to his Highness regarding the welfare of the dogs. Whereupon the Secretary put his fist through a window by way of easing his feelings, and started on the return journey to the Palace, which he reached at 11 P.M., to be told that his Highness had been assured by some one else of the safe arrival of the dogs and would not require to see him that night, but would expect him early in the morning!

We stayed a fortnight after the visitors left, as we were invited to go to camp with the Royal Family. It is said that if man knew at the beginning of a venture what he did at the end, there would be no cause for repenting. That applied to us at the end of the fortnight.

We left with bag and baggage for the first camp, which we reached by car. The roads to that camp must have been unmapped. We went through rivers and farmers' fields and stuck dozens of times in waterholes. We were bumped mercilessly. Six of us sat in a four-seater; the spare room somebody evidently thought existed was taken up by four large dogs. The inside of the car was like a furnace. The windows had to be kept shut on account of the dogs.

Arrived at last, we found everything beautifully arranged, our tent being next to the Rajah's, and the others in two rows reaching for a quarter of a mile on either side of the newly made road.

The first trouble arose when it was found out that the Secretary had been considerately treated by being given a double-fly tent; the whole of the Hindu staff went on strike at the discovery of preference being given to a Muslim. A durbar was called at midday, for his Highness had intimated that he was not disposed to conduct any business of State before that hour. He sat looking thoroughly disgruntled, drinking ovaltine (the doctor having forbidden anything stronger) while the A.D.C.s stood first on one foot, then on the other. Everybody looked either at the tent ceiling or the ground. After the fourth cup of ovaltine the Rajah decided that it was badly made and sent for the Italian cook—a temperamental and well-meaning man, whose dignity was sorely injured by being brought to book before the whole camp, and who, when the interview was over, burst into tears and later took to his bed, suffering violently from the disgrace, which brought on a fever. He was only cured when the next day he was sent for by his employer, cried anew copiously, and was comforted sufficiently by his master to allow his work to continue. It all seemed very childish to me.

The first night in camp was pay-day for the A.D.C.s, whose previous two months' wages had long ago been lost at cards. Some well-checked excitement which one could readily understand was evident in their ranks. As pay-time drew near, they were even noticed to have departed so far from the allowed freedom as to be kicking stones behind the Royal quarters. This hilarity was soon stopped, for one of the guards looked for but a fleeting second fiercely in their direction. Now none of the guards was going to risk his life by being accused of neglect of duty—arduous as that duty was, for each person requiring to enter the Royal tent had to be challenged and questioned regarding his business. Even those who had stuck to their guns for twenty years did not escape. Our tent was uncomfortably near to the Royal one, possibly a sore point with Hindu guests, and it was not an uncommon occurrence to be awakened by a shout which proved to be but the sentry's challenge. The Rajah was deaf, a fact which probably accounted for the loudness of the challenge and the sentry's total disregard of the noise he made when he cleared his throat and expectorated with violence at the end of his twenty paces—which was, unfortunately, directly behind where I slept.

Pay was given out by the Secretary together with

orders for the A.D.C.s to be ready for cards after dinner. How quickly are hopes dashed! No more stone-kicking behind the camp for probably another two months! Dinner over, the Rajah proceeded with his guests to where the card-tables were laid out and the victims already standing at attention for what must have been to them pure sacrifice. Half-way through the evening his Highness suddenly noticed that the light from one of the hanging lamps struck directly into his eyes. The play stopped until the man responsible for the tragedy was brought. He proved to be an old servant whose one crime this had been in thirty years. Being able to give no suitable reason for his misdemeanour, for by the State law no one ever dared excuse himself, he was ordered to leave Dumpur the next day. He approached an official regarding the three months' pay due to him, but was told that such a small detail could not be brought to the Rajah's attention at such an inauspicious moment, nor would the Secretary act in the matter without instructions. The lamp was re-hung, and although it would have been an infinitely more simple matter to move the card-table, no one seemed willing to make the suggestion in the Royal presence.

An hour later the A.D.C.s were losing as steadily as before. I was unable to discover whether their continuous misfortune was due to pure bad play or to their belief that it would hardly be etiquette for them to win money from the Rajah's guests. Doubtless the visitors were unaware of the A.D.C.s' status and ignorant of the havoc wrought in these twenty officials' finances by the result of the evening's play. At 1 A.M. the Rajah rose from his seat, delighted by the evident success of the entertainment and the pleasure of his guests, and, receiving the floor-sweeping salaams of the company, he walked to his tent. Behind him came the winners, in great good humour, and bringing up the rear were the unfortunate losers, whose woebegone faces made a pathetic sight.

Next day a very highly placed British Government official arrived to spend two days at *shikar*. The whole of that day the camp buzzed like a beehive; everything had to be perfect for the eyes of the visitor not only in the camp but at the Palace. Relays of messengers were sent between the two places carrying orders, as new ideas for further improvement came to the minds of those who were responsible. One of the couriers was found in a collapsed condition at midnight, having made the journey twelve times in such haste that he had no time even for quenching his thirst.

The Secretary reported late that night that all was as his Highness desired—even the 'untouchable' *bungi* (sweeper) had a clean loincloth, in case the great Sahib should chance to see him. A special tent was prepared, of large proportions and corresponding comfort. The best pieces of furniture were borrowed from our tents, and I hope the visitor fully appreciated my feather-bed and mattress, for, although my private offer of it no doubt preserved some one's position in the household, its loss certainly caused me two nights of unusual discomfort.

The official wanted to shoot only one day, and the difficulty arose as to how he was to be entertained the second day. A proposal that he should be shown over the Royal kennels was unanimously adopted, and the Secretary telephoned to the guest's secretary, asking if this met with his master's approval. It did, and the State Secretary was ordered to see that all went smoothly, and was informed that on no account was any unfavourable impression to be gained by the distinguished visitor. These officials pay yearly visits for the British Government and report how the States progress. Their post is no sinecure.

The Royal car containing the official and the Secretary arrived the next afternoon at the kennels. The whole night had been spent having the dogs brushed and prepared, but the officer-in-charge, being accustomed to irregular hours, was uncomplaining. The guest expressed the greatest delight and satisfaction at all he saw—as he would have done at less personal sacrifice to all concerned. Just as he was leaving, a small pup attracted his attention and, bending down, he took it in his arms and remarked how much he liked it. The Secretary, slightly flushed with the unaccustomed praise and his success, and wishing to round off the day as he felt sure his Highness would approve, said he knew the Rajah would be honoured if the guest would accept the puppy. The official was delighted and expressed his gratitude.

Now it so happened that this puppy was one of a litter which had been advertised for sale in the local newspaper. The incident had been observed and was reported to higher quarters. The officer-in-charge, whose zealous devotion to his master's interests on this occasion outstripped his discretion, immediately made out a bill for fifty rupees and presented it to the British guest, having meanwhile informed the Rajah that this satisfactory sale had been accomplished. The position was highly embarrassing. The Secretary was deeply ashamed and disgusted that an honoured guest had been so treated, yet he did not dare either to bring the real facts before the Rajah or to offer an apology to the visitor.

The two nights the British official had spent at the camp were models of the perfect life. There was wine of nearly every kind on the table, but his Highness drank only water. Meal-time was usually brightened considerably by the Royal wit, but it seemed strangely missing then. Those two dinners were not very much enjoyed by anybody, for the guests feared the glum look of their host, and, as the incident of the sacred fish had lost nothing in the telling, the time was given chiefly to retrospection. The chief guest, who sat on my right, must have considered me either slightly under the influence of drink or simply reserved. But I felt under a cloud, for I was afraid that the Rajah, knowing that I too was British by birth, would think I would be likely to report to my fellow-countryman anything that might have displeased me. Luckily I overheard the Under-Secretary and another employee, who both spoke English, talking about this while I was dressing for dinner. They had forgotten it was easy to hear through the tent, or perhaps thought I was out. Not wanting to hear any more I called out: "Who is there?" Quick as lightning came the reply that a dog was lost and they apologized for making so much noise looking for him. "I certainly think you are in the right tent, in any case," I could not help replying.

The next night, after the visitor had gone, his Highness regained his wit, and we were amused throughout the meal. I daresay I should not have laughed at all the jokes if etiquette had not required me to join in the general mirth.

With the departure of the rather embarrassing guest, things returned to their normal round. The feather-bed returned to me and the sweeper reassumed his usual grubbiness.

The order was now given for a departure to the next *shikar* some miles away. Men were sent ahead as usual to erect a complete village of tents. Those we occupied were dismantled and made ready for the move. After many animated discussions we were packed again into the car, to plough through more and worse fields, rivers, and waterholes. We came across a staff car containing six of the Ranee's maidservants stuck in mid-stream. The river was too deep to wade, and no repairs could be done under the water. The car looked in a hopeless condition, and was no match for the Ranee's colossal companion, who weighed at least eighteen stone. An elephant bearing some of the *shikaris* now came along, and the rescue of the marooned maids seemed more likely. While the rescue men were willing to help carry the servants to the bank, it was noticeable that the fat woman was left in the car. No volunteers were forthcoming —not unnaturally, for none of the men was beyond average height and, after all, they had their own safety to think of. They dared not use the elephant as a tow, as there was nobody empowered to give orders. Meanwhile, the fat woman decided that anything was better than uncertainty and proceeded to relieve herself of all unnecessary clothing. This proved too much for some of the male onlookers, who suddenly found they were late and left us the poorer by six men. A small man—an ex-major of the British Army, who was acting as a sort of companion-secretary-entertainer to the Rajah—feeling that though no longer in the employment of his country he was not debarred from remaining a gentleman, gallantly stepped forward and offered himself as rescuer. The sight would have caused roars of laughter on a movie screen, but this was reality. The result was only too apparent from the start, and within the next few minutes the little man, up to the waist in the now muddy water, was grappling with his burden. Things were going wonderfully well—too well, for a false step lost the ex-major his foothold, and both were deposited with a tremendous splash in the water. It was a moment fraught with terror, for the little man was nowhere to be seen. I turned away, as I was packed too tightly in the car to have extricated myself in the haste now required if a rescue was to be effected in time. A great rushing of feet past our car resulted in the two being dragged out more dead than alive. The rest of the uncomfortable journey was forgotten by those of us who thanked our lucky stars that we were at least dry.

At the next camp late nights were followed by mornings which might have been glorious had not our neighbour in the next tent devoted quite an hour to a part of his religion requiring much gargling and more noise. I was beginning to dislike this worship which started so early and demonstratively just as we were having our *chota hazri* (early tea). Even the explanation of the necessity, which follows, scarcely made me think of my neighbour's nasal ablutions in a less hostile way.

In days long past, it is said, an Afghan conqueror, Mahmud of Ghazni, descended on India. He had little difficulty in quelling the Hindus, but was not so successful in separating them from their idols, which he found they continued to worship in private. Though he had an intense hatred for idols, he thought the devotion of the Hindus required a fitting and lasting 'tribute.' So, unknown to any of that faith, he gave orders for one of their huge idols to be ground to the finest powder, which was then mixed with dried *dal* (lentils) and sold to the Hindus in the bazaars. All unsuspecting, the idol-worshippers ate their god, and only when that adulterated consignment of *dal* was finished to the last grain did Mahmud of Ghazni speak. That started the fatal gargling which has gone on through the centuries and is so faithfully carried out, for the Hindu sage said that the only way to get the last holy grain out of the throat was to gargle as long as a Hindu was left to carry out the command.

CHAPTER XIV

THE RAJAH'S TREASURE

THE festivities were now over and the guests had departed. We alone remained in Dumpur State. His Highness would not hear of our going. We had travelled so far, he said, and had yet to see much of the State life. Candidly I had seen enough of it. The narrow unoccupied lives of the Ranee and Princesses, who seemed only to go in and out of the rooms to food or sleep as the case might be, drove me almost to distraction.

Day after day the Ranee sat watching while I taught her companion to steer a clear way through the intricacies of knitting and crochet. When they saw me sketching they would not be satisfied until I taught one of the 'hangers-on' to paint and draw so that he might be of more use to the Rajah! It was not an easy matter to put years of practice into a few weeks' lessons.

One day, forgetting the rules of the State, my husband beat his Highness at tennis. This cast a gloom over the whole State! Employees stood about in knots discussing the unprecedented circumstance. At last the Chief Minister found a solution. The marker had made a mistake; the rogue ought to be dismissed. His Highness was so delighted with the childish explanation that he told the man he might remain if such a thing never happened again! This smoothed over, life went on in the same way. Every night the Rajah held a durbar to hear the report of each man's work for that day. As this always took place after dinner the Rajah often went to sleep during the hearing, and since no one dared to disturb him the durbar sometimes went on until 3 A.M. The wretched employees were obliged to get up at 6 A.M. sharp, so that they often had little sleep. Each servant kept an eagle eye on his neighbour in order to be able to report any mis-doing and so gain Royal favour and, what was dearer, promotion.

The ex-major previously mentioned justified his position at the Court by doing anything his Highness asked. Sometimes he was required to sing and play; sometimes he dressed as an English butler when a guest of importance who had an English manservant visited the State. Once we were amazed to see him walking about arrayed as a typical John Bull, who was introduced to a Persian guest as "the Duke of England, the King-Emperor's son." The guest was duly impressed and called the major "Your Highness."

The elder Princess celebrated her twenty-first birthday while we were there, and a large cake for the occasion was made by the French pastry-cook. Many guests were invited for a few days' stay and on the birthday a very large tea-party was given. When the cake was cut we were amused to find the usual silver trumperies that please grown-ups as well as children. Margaret, who was a special favourite and always sat beside his Highness, found a two-anna piece (smaller than a threepenny piece, silver, and valued at twopence). She was delighted with it and held it up for us all to see. Presently a servant came with a tray and asked us to put on it what we had found. We thought there must be a joke somewhere, but the worthless little objects were removed and never seen again. Margaret wept long and loudly at her loss, but was pacified with a rupee which his Highness asked Syed to give to the child.

The Rajah was a keen connoisseur of precious gems and was always anxious to add to his collection. One night I persuaded him to take us to see the State jewels. He very reluctantly agreed, and the next evening, when no other amusement had been provided, he collected ten guards with rifles and drawn swords and took us across the Palace yard some hundred yards to the strong-room, which was within a specially built house. Twenty guards stood outside and loudly challenged us. His Highness was so pleased at such a great show of attention to duty that he ordered the men to be given four annas each (fourpence). They must have known quite well who was coming, as the surrounding area was brightly lighted for the visitors.

The great outer door required many keys to open it, bolts had to be slid back, then a patent spring was touched. As soon as we were inside, with ten guards with drawn swords, the great door was banged to—Aladdin must have felt exactly as we did.

Electric lights blazed instantly all over the

place. We were not, it appeared, in the strong-room yet, for pretty much the same performance had to be gone through again. I began to wonder why the twenty guards were stationed outside, for no man could possibly have got into that stronghold in any ordinary life-time. Once again more lights were switched on, another door was opened, and at last we were there. The room was full of old silver armour set with gems, coats of mail diamond-studded, helmets with huge rubies, glass cases lined with white, blue, and purple velvet, on which blazed gems like living fire. It was breath-taking—I looked round in utter amazement. Great solid gold vases inlaid with diamonds; goblets encrusted with rubies; cups and saucers of solid silver; gemmed footstools; pipes, caps, dozens of ruby, sapphire, and pearl studs; clocks, watches, bracelets, rings, ear-rings, gold shoes with diamond-studded heels, sapphire-studded spurs, whips, saddles, and twenty-two gorgeously jewelled outfits for elephants, each (his Highness said) worth £50,000!

The room scintillated. There were boxes, six feet by four feet, which were a mass of blazing gems. One case contained loose pearls, another diamonds of all sizes, another rubies, another sapphires, another opals. There were walking-sticks encrusted with jewels, worth thousands of pounds; armchairs with every inch covered with pearls and diamonds, with footstools to match. A solid gold dinner-service, with gold cutlery, had been made by the Rajah's orders after he had returned from a European visit. Having heard that the King-Emperor had a gold service, he decided to improve upon it by having his jewelled.

I do not know how long we had been there when I fingered my pearl necklace, a very humble thing although I had always been very proud of it. On the spur of the moment I remarked how much I valued it. The Rajah looked intently at it for a few minutes, then said, "May I see it?"

"Certainly," I replied.

"These are strangely beautiful pearls."

"They are Scottish pearls, found in the rivers at home."

"I have no Scottish pearls and shall not rest now until I have. Why has this been overlooked by my Chief Minister?" That official, who was accompanying us, wilted under the Rajah's rebuke and obviously determined to make good his omission at the earliest opportunity.

As we were leaving I noticed some plain sandalwood boxes, the scent of which filled the room. They were as large as big trunks.

"Yes, you must see these."

"What a pity to hide them away here," I said.

"Well, we cannot very well allow them to lie about," replied the Rajah, as he beckoned to two of the men to open one of the boxes.

"You see, there are a few stones here."

That box was filled with precious stones; his Highness dug his hands into them and allowed them to fall through his fingers, like a stream of water sparkling in the sunlight. I felt cold and hot alternately at the sight. The other box contained more jewels. His Highness said he had never seen the bottom of those boxes and probably never would!

While in that strong-room the idea of the simple things of life faded away. One could think only in terms of precious stones. I could not help contrasting the vast wealth stored in this room with the terrible poverty of most Indian villages.

Next morning as I was dressing Ahmed came to say the Chief Minister wanted to see me urgently. I wondered whether I were suspected of taking any jewels the night before, and naked swords passed before my mind. In the drawing-room of the guest-house I found the Chief Minister pacing up and down.

"I have come on a painful duty," he began. My knees grew weak; I felt chilled with fear.

"Yes," I stuttered.

"You remember last night, Begum Sahiba."

"Yes, distinctly," I replied.

"Do you recollect an incident of the pearls?"

"The pearls? No!"

"Think," he encouraged, glossily, rubbing his palms together.

"What pearls? His Highness's pearls?" I shook as I said the words. "Please tell me what is wrong."

"Well, my master greatly admired your Scottish pearls, the first he has ever seen, and asked me to inquire when you would care to give him any—er—information about them."

"Do you mean he wants the address of a Scottish jeweller? I can give you the name of a very reliable one."

"Of course we do not like to trouble you. Perhaps you might care to donate the pearls you have to the collection of his Highness."

"I am sorry I cannot. They are very precious to me, for sentimental reasons."

"Of course, I quite understand," he replied to my great relief.

It is worth while to mention here a strange sequel to this incident. We had heard that jewel-thieves abounded in the neighbourhood—the Rajah's own precautions for the safety of his treasure-house showed the truth of this—and shortly afterwards I awoke one morning to find that my necklace had vanished, though it had been secured round my neck with a double spring catch when I had gone to bed.

A few days later we said good-bye to the Rajah and went to visit a Muslim Nawab who lived near Delhi. His son had been a student at a Scottish university and was Syed's friend. I must confess that I breathed a sigh of relief when after a short railway journey we reached the Nawab's house, where we were given an entire wing of seven rooms to ourselves.

CHAPTER XV

THE MAGIC SODA-WATER MACHINE

IT was the first thing I saw on my return from an early morning ride a few days later. It was the first thing I was intended to see as I stepped into the veranda. It lay prominently on the table beside my newspapers, held down determinedly by a glass paper-weight.

Had it come by post it would probably have been thrown on one side and forgotten, but the slight unconventionality in the manner of leaving it attracted me.

The green pamphlet embellished with red and purple informed me that "the most great sale about to take place, in which all material of the noble army at present in station and leaving within a few short days for up-country to be disposed off. Only this as being the cause for sale at the which anyone requiring of saddels for horses, blankets, stables furnitures and many more valuable affects much numberless to mention ought to be there on Friday as the gates opined."

Criticize the English if you like: it was the best that the Hindu *babu* could do.

Friday then, as the "gates opined," I was there, and was greatly surprised to see a large gathering. All the available seats were occupied.

The gaze of the Hindu gate-keeper followed mine.

"You see, mighty lady, these people were here since four hours. I not know how to do all about my sixpence entrance going." The bulky Pathans paid neither money nor attention, but just strode in.

"Why not ask for payment?" I proposed to the gate-keeper, noticing his predicament.

"I asking, but sahibs getting angry, saying I not at gate when arriving. They not giving. Telling me going bad places."

A good start for the "most great sale"! Luckily, my servant brought a camp-chair for me, albeit from the lot to be auctioned, but one is not expected to know everything.

The early arrivals were calling for water and employing anyone within sight who looked like a servant. The large field looked as though it would be required.

Sweet- and fruit-sellers began to arrive. Their offer of eightpence[1] on the way out instead of the sixpence entrance as per pamphlet was not accepted by the gate-keeper, who argued loud and pointedly. Eventually he accepted fourpence entrance and sixpence on the way out. I had a feeling that their exit would not be past Babu Jee, the gate-keeper, as I had noticed one or two holes torn by boys through the matting wall held fast with bamboo sticks. He seemed to think so himself, for he looked searchingly at them as though committing their features to memory for future reference.

[1] For convenience I give in this chapter the English equivalent of the various Indian sums.

Their number swelled. News travels far and fast when there is a reduction in prices, and the gate-keeper began to regret his weakness in allowing the first contingent to pass, and flatly refused to let any more enter without full payment. Just as the various sellers and hawkers began to make the passage for anxious arrivals difficult, another stalwart Pathan arrived at the gate. All immediately made way for the huge hill-man armed with the usual big stick.

Once inside he soon dispersed the faint-hearted fruit-sellers already admitted, who returned to protest against the invasion of those who would so considerably reduce their profit. The Pathan, however, waved these in past the feebly protesting *babu* and immediately began to help himself from their baskets. When they saw no money was forthcoming from their champion, who pointed out that, having paid no entrance fee, there could be no loss to them, they would have returned even as they came, but, as the Pathan had walked off with the end of his turban filled with fruit, Babu Jee refused to let them out unless they paid sixpence according to the previous arrangement. There was no choice but to proceed.

The gathering had now grown to a dense crowd. The auction was about to begin—at least, the two soldiers walking along behind a bell-ringer seemed to signify the commencement.

It was even so. A saddle was held up for the first bid. "Fine saddle," announced Tommy. "Cost twenty-eight pounds, belonged to the Major. What offers?"

Bidding began at sixpence and leaped to two pounds after a minute. The field was now held by two bidders who glared at each other menacingly as the price rose. "Two pounds ten," roared the tall one with the hennaed beard, aiming a look of triumph at his adversary, who remained silent.

"Fifty shillings! Any advance? It's a gift!" prompted the second Tommy.

"It is," exultantly replied the bearded one, applauding himself loudly.

The next lot was a set of collapsing aluminium tumblers. Tommy knew his audience.

"Look," he called. "Here is a small dish, press this and you'll see it is a tumbler! How is that? The same with the others—six of them! What offers for these English tumblers, all the way from Walayat—England?"

Now I knew these were for sale in Indian-owned English shops for about two shillings, and Tommy knew it too. The audience did not, for murmurs of "Angraisi tumbler" and "magic cup" reached my ears. The awe of being in the presence of such a wonder was felt by all. The bidding started at ten shillings. What else would you expect for a magic cup all the way from England? Up and up went the price to a pound! A good English pound!

Just then the arrival of a prominent member of cantonment society in the presence of the Nawab of Kanda, our host—though that was not his real name—brought the majority to their feet and the salute. His tall figure, set off by a wonderful flowing gold-embroidered cloak and an imposing-looking sword in a richly jewelled scabbard, was but fitting to the occasion. His bodyguard ranged itself round him as he took the seat of honour in the front row, and the bidding continued. I kept out of sight on the end seat.

"One pound," shouted Tommy. "Look here, this 'ere magic tumbler is the only one of its kind in India! And going for a pound. I'll buy it meself!"

Magic tumbler! The words caught the ears of the Nawab. The case was passed along. His Highness could not open the small cup. Tommy was at once in attendance; lemonade was brought so that the demonstration might be complete. "Two pounds," came from the seat of honour in the front row. "Two pounds ten," from a few rows behind.

The Nawab sat up, stroked the handle of his sword—his ancestors had not been Pathans for nothing—and glared backward in the hope of detecting his outbidder.

"Two pounds ten shillings for six magic tumblers? A give-away!" continued the perspiring auctioneer.

"Five pounds," thundered the Nawab. Silence followed. He would have been a brave man who would have broken it, even if he had felt justified.

A commotion now arose in a near part of the field. It was only Babu Jee selecting some more fruit as rebate for having allowed the fruit-sellers in on reduced terms.

A collection of what looked like old spurs and broken reins and whips was now being bid for.

"Look, all this, enough for twenty horses, for the price of six pounds!" encouraged Tommy No. 1, while his brother auctioneer drank deeply and deservingly from a bottle in the rear.

It was evident that those placed in full view of the bundle now being auctioned held their peace and perhaps learned a lesson. It was also evident there was some rivalry in the back rows, less favourably placed. The last bid was two pounds.

"Look at this silver-handled whip; belonged to the Viceroy at one time." I could see that the lash was missing, and no explanation was offered as to the occasion on which the Viceroy required a carriage horse-whip.

"Four pounds," called the Nawab amid roars of approval of lesser lights. The assembly had divided itself into two camps—one in favour of the seat of honour and one upholding the back rows.

The look Tommy No. 1 gave Tommy No. 2 as the bid was clinched might have been due to my imagination, but the amusing way Tommy No. 2 urged him on in 'gora' language—white soldiers' lingo—was certainly not.

A halt was now called and lemonade was passed round. Nawab Sahib would only drink from the magic tumbler. Slight consternation occurred while this was brought and washed. Fruit-, sweet-, and lemonade-sellers did good work. It was getting rather warm now, and relays of lemonade and soda-water began to appear at the gate leading to the field. The Pathan had been joined by several brother hill-men, who were speedily teaching three fruit-sellers the blessings of doing the right thing at a wrong moment. Four lemonade-sellers were in exclusive attendance upon the Nawab. It was not every day that a magic tumbler was sold, let alone six, and "it was wonderful," the owner of these was heard to say, "being the possessor of these marvels, how much more lemonade it was possible to enjoy!"

" 'Ere we 'ave a number of horse blankets in good condition, bound in good 'ard-wearin' tape and all in A1 condition."

I did not care for the way the Tommies had juggled with the blankets during the interval, but I was not buying them.

A feeble voice offered six shillings.

"Listen, ladies and gents and Nabobs, six shillings for these, like the Commander-in-Chief's."

"Twenty," a voice called far back in the crowd.

"Twenty!" repeated Tommy with sarcasm, glorying in having met his vocation in life at last. "Is this a bid you would expect from this gatherin'?"

"Thirty," boomed another voice.

"Thirty, for these 'ere first-class blankets, taped? And look at the initials, the proof they can't be beat."

The majority of the vast audience might have noticed in less exciting moments that the initials were those of the regiment, but the general atmosphere pervading even an ordinary auction—which this was not—makes clear thought difficult.

"A hundred," came the now easily recognized voice of Nawab Sahib.

For the briefest of moments Tommy lost any previous belief he might have possessed regarding his hearing.

"A hundred, any advance?" Advance, I believe, from the back seats would have caused a riot. Luckily there was none.

Proceedings were now closed while the purchases of Nawab Sahib were being transferred from the auction platform to a space near the front row, where they lay as a warning to any future bidder that his choice would not easily be realized.

The carriage of Kanda now drew up outside the gate. It was but the work of a few seconds to give the order for its dismissal, after which the Nawab sank down in his chair. Not for him to desert his field! The bidders looked the disappointment they felt at this turn of affairs. Even the man with the hennaed beard began to realize that the fifty-shilling saddle alone was going to be his share in this record-breaking sale, and chewed fiercely and noisily at the betel-nut he was munching.

A consignment of pails and buckets was next held up. Eyelet-holes of blue sky showed through the majority that would bear even distant inspection. This in no way affected the bidding, which rose by leaps from sixpence to thirty shillings—a few more than they would have cost new. I knew that the Nawab was bidding to show the gathering that he still was a big personality. His prestige as a landlord—*the* landlord—was at stake.

"Any more offers for these 'ere buckets?" shouted Tommy, who was becoming hoarse, while he looked hopefully to where previously his appeals had been so successful. But Nawab Sahib was having a nap, and the man who had offered thirty shillings had since bidding either had my view of the pails or regretted his ardour, and up they went again, to be knocked down for forty shillings.

Several hundred pairs of army boots, bundles of regulation shirts in fives, and tunics that owed nobody anything, were disposed of. All the while, the occupant of the front seat remained in, but not of, the gathering. A soft cool air was blowing through the leaves of the giant pepal tree under which the auction was in progress.

Both auctioneers had removed coats and waistcoats, and rolled up their sleeves as if about to enter a boxing-ring. They were out to sell these lots and would see it done!

It was only when a huge machine for making soda-water was put up that the Nawab of Kanda awoke.

"What bid for this 'ere sody-water machine?" There was considerable shuffling; everybody looked at everybody else, and finally all gazed at the Nawab, but there was never a bid.

"This 'ere machine makes sody-water in a minute, one man can work it. Why buy sody-water when you can make your own?" went on Tommy, warming to the subject. His remarks as usual were translated to all bidders. They were agreed to by all—then followed by a long murmur of many voices, the purport of which could not be determined.

"Would it be possible to see the working perhaps?" ventured one engaged in the business of a flourishing restaurant.

"Hi, you show this blighter how she works," Tommy called to his friend with relief in his voice.

"Where is he first?" asked the demonstrator. "Oh! it's that Swiss-Italiano from Kirkcaldy. Never! I'm coming."

Tommy No. 2 crawled from somewhere behind, and with the help of his friend and three loafers the machine was pushed into the full view of the bidders. Some quick work of pressing and lever-moving produced a stoppered bottle of soda-water. A murmur of awed surprise arose from the assembly. Some ventured near, others held well back from the miracle. Tommy stood as though he alone had been responsible for the feat of producing both the machine and the soda-water.

It was not the time to ask for bids, and Tommy knew it.

"Ladies and gents, I now propose to allow you to taste this soda-water."

Never, every one agreed, had soda-water of such a singularly delicious flavour been tasted. Every tongue was loosened, and, the first shock over, the conversation began anew. Past events were past, even the magic tumblers were forgotten. Knots of people gathered together to discuss the marvel of the day—this magic machine that produced soda-water inside a bottle complete with a stopper!

Tommy, guessing the tide to be at its highest point, called for bids.

"You have to-day, ladies and gents, seen with your own eyes this wonderful machine." Applause. "I now ask you to offer me a bid, and need to 'ardly say this machine will pay its way within a few weeks."

"Fifty shillings!" called Tommy's Swiss-Italiano.

Up the bidding went almost by the shilling, until a hundred had been reached. The Italian had exhausted the utmost possibilities of his purse.

"A 'undred shillings for a machine that makes sody-water for nothing and cost a thousand—and only used to make the sody-water the Colonel Sahib has at bed-time! Doctor's orders!"

It was not the Colonel Sahib who drank soda-water at bed-time, for I knew him well; but I realized that Tommy had to dispose of the machine, and the Colonel to his mind was somebody to be reckoned with.

This caused the bidding to go up to a hundred and fifty.

"It makes me 'eart ache to let this machine go for a 'undred and fifty, and if I 'ad the money——" but what Tommy would have felt called upon to do had he possessed the wherewithal must remain unrecorded, for a yell from the front row announced that the Nawab would take it as it stood for two hundred and fifty shillings.

Smiles wreathed the faces of the auctioneers. "Friday, the thirteenth, my lucky day!" he called to his friend, who, less experienced than the seller of the machine, began to explain the difficulty there might be with some particular part.

"Have you bought this 'ere concern?" asked auctioneer No. 1.

"No fear."

"Then mind yer own bisniss and shut up."

Meanwhile a messenger was sent post-haste for two bullock-carts to remove the acquisitions of the

Nawab. Tommy began to sing: "Send me a letter from your garden." The field began to clear. Nawab Sahib sat on. It was strange how the way of exit, even of those in the back rows, led past *the* chair in the front row.

The gazes of half-admiration, half-amazement were, however, lost on the Nawab, who must have been populating a world where a machine was going to make soda-water for him for ever.

A bullock-cart is a worthy vehicle but not a speedy one, and it was two hours later that two drew up almost beside where the only chair now remaining contained the fairy godfather of the auction. The rest of the auction scene had vanished and only the Nawab and his retainers remained.

The next hour was fraught with terrible moments, as the wonder machine was loaded with care on to the cart, and quantities of dried grass were packed round it. The Nawab alone issued commands as these sacred rites were being performed. When the cart was laden with the machine, the order was given for the bullocks to proceed slowly (which was not needed) and carefully (which undoubtedly was). With great effort the cart eventually reached the road, led by the driver and followed by the Nawab's bodyguard on foot. The Kanda carriage with the Nawab thereof and myself followed in the rear.

To those who had participated in the auction the return home of the magic machine was understood, if not sympathized with. A line, almost a guard of honour, had formed along the road to the house. To some who had not been to the auction the singular sight was amusing. Several times the procession drew up to make sure all was well with the soda-water machine.

Once home, several altercations were entered into before a suitable place could be found for it. It was scarcely an ornament and yet it could not be put in the kitchen. A joiner was summoned to build a roof and walls round it in the orchard.

The next part of the programme was the proposal of a house-warming in honour of the new acquisition. No invitation was refused, and the party was a large one. Only after the guests arrived was the discovery made that the man who was supposed to understand the making of the soda-water had either never known or forgotten. The favoured plan was to send for the auctioneer. But the reply was that Tommy had left with his regiment the day before. Lemonade was brought from the bazaar and the party went on in a half-hearted manner until it broke up.

The difficulty now remained to get a man who understood the working of it. The story that this soda-water machine had never yet been understood by anybody gained strength, and I remembered soda-water being brought on the day of the auction to the two auctioneers, who had complained greatly of thirst, and again when the machine was alleged to have made soda-water for the teetotal Colonel. However, one does not say these things to people who have bought articles one never had any faith in or one merely becomes unpopular; and popularity must be maintained at all costs!

A few weeks of dread uncertainty followed, when

people called to inquire after the soda-water machine much as they would if any member of the household had developed measles, and the time came when the very mention of the unfortunate purchase wrenched a sigh, for all the world as if a tender foot had been trodden upon.

Things were at their very worst when news came, nobody knew how—nobody ever does know how—of a man in Lahore who knew everything from A to Z about a soda-water machine.

A servant was at once dispatched to persuade this unique specimen of humanity that it would be to his considerable advantage to remove to Kanda and man the machine. The great one had never been far from Lahore in his life, and it took the utmost offer in wages—ten pounds monthly (a cook receives but two)—to persuade him to go to Kanda.

The obstacles did not end here. It appeared the man had a wife and family whom he could not be expected to leave for all the soda-water machines in the world. The invitation to bring his family was accepted, with fares paid. The man arrived just as advance preparations were being made to spend a few months in another house belonging to Kanda some distance away. He therefore proposed that he should take the machine and fix it up there.

The deep insight of the newcomer was commented upon and admired. The lucky man who had heard of him was congratulated, and a peace such as had not been known since the day of the auction stole over Kanda. With immense care the machine was taken to pieces by the new engineer in order that it might be packed. Orders were freely given that he was to have all the assistance required in both men and money.

Followed the day when the bullock-cart was loaded once more with the precious machine, accompanied by the engineer, and followed by a second bullock-cart containing his family. The ceremony of its departure was only equalled by that of its original arrival at Kanda. More orders as to the mode of procedure were given. The journey was to be by easy stages, which totalled up to something like a day's travel and a day's rest, all expenses of food and lodging being defrayed.

Anxiety was keenly felt by all, until a letter arrived announcing the safe arrival of both bullock conveyances. The relief following the days of strain was so great that several members of the family almost collapsed.

The arrival of the postman was now the only link with the wonder machine. Every day letters were written and read to the family so that any point not fully understood might be further elucidated. Nevertheless, no member of the family would have dared to offer any suggestions.

The day the letter came to say that, the shed having been erected, the machine was about to be built in, four telegrams containing instructions of warning and orders that the latest developments were to be reported daily left the house before the postmaster was out of his bed. The natural request that some money should be sent, as a little was required immediately, met with the generous response of a month's wages in advance and something over for running expenses.

All this time the family had refrained from leaving Kanda. A set day soon comes, and excitement ran high when a letter was received from the engineer announcing his complete readiness and satisfaction with the entire affair. In two days the family was ready for the journey.

We eventually arrived, tired and hungry but excited as school-children. After having something to eat, the first thing was to see the new soda-water machine. The engineer was sent for, but could not be found. Faithful man! Of course, he would be in the machine-shed.

Where was the machine-shed? None of the servants knew what we were referring to. The head cook said a man had spent a few weeks there, declaring that he had been given permission by the Nawab to go on leave on account of poor health. The cook expressed the greatest surprise on hearing of a soda-water machine. There had never been such a thing there, and the man left after he had received a telegraphed sum of money which he was awaiting anxiously.

That, then, was the end of the magic machine, and all inquiries brought the same reply—nobody knew. Whether the local policeman had anything to do with the get-away will never be known. In any case, he had full responsibility of all investigation. We discovered long afterwards that he was the brother of the engineer—and no man is his brother's keeper!

CHAPTER XVI

THROUGH NINETY-NINE TUNNELS

WE spent a month with the Nawab and saw all the sights of Delhi. My father-in-law was now anxious for us to return to the hill-country, being probably afraid we were becoming 'idol-worshippers' in Hindustan. So we promised to start the journey after the hot season, which was just beginning and would continue without mercy in the Plains for the best part of six months. We were also anxious to see the Simla hills, of which we had heard so much, and it was necessary to escape the heat.

Towards the end of February the English mem-sahibs are seen less and less in their verandas and clubs in the Plains. During the 'cold weather' from September until February you can walk out during the day from 9 A.M. right through the afternoon. From March until the end of August this is impossible owing to the scorching heat or the torrential monsoon rains, and no Englishwoman who can afford to do otherwise spends the hot season in the Plains.

The verandas are the popular rendezvous for one's friends at all hours during the winter season, and empty verandas signify that the women are packing for the hills, where they probably have houses or will live in the hotels. As it will be six months before one returns and all sorts of weather will be experienced in the hills, one must find room for everything, including mattresses, bedclothes, china, cutlery, and all the kitchen utensils.

In the last few days before the exodus, as I tried in vain to find somewhere to eat an ice before it became but a plate of over-sweetened warmish milk, I thought of the worldly paradise awaiting me in the hills and steeled myself against the discomfort we were suffering.

I saw the last box being well and truly sat upon by the entire kitchen staff and miraculously closed. Khansama (cook) reported that all the kitchen utensils were corded and that when the dish-cloths (which were hanging up) were dry his packing would be done. My bearer assured me in broken English:

"All memsahib's clothes tied up!"

"All packed?" I asked doubtfully.

"Yes, Huzoor."

The reply did not satisfy me. Some things are too good to be true.

"Go and make sure, and if there is anything over bring it here."

Ten minutes later he brought a pack of things requiring at least three expanding cases.

Although it was hot when we left Delhi, we were told to expect to see snow on the ground when we reached the height of eight thousand feet. Hence we were to start in summer clothes and dress warmly on the way, keeping fur coats and even snow-boots in the train compartment!

"Are the thick coats we require for our arrival in Simla left out?"

No, of course they would not be. As a matter of fact the box in which they were packed had left an hour previously on the advance luggage bullock-cart which was lumbering on its way to the station.

A boy had to be sent to open the box and retrieve the coats. The heat was now unbearable—the bearer threw cold water on to the closely woven grass curtain to make the room cooler. I left the perspiring staff and lay down under a mosquito net—too thirsty almost to call for water. I must have drunk fifty glasses of iced water that day. The head bearer sent a message to the second to tell the third to bring an iced drink. "Tinkle tinkle" sounded the ice against the side of the glass as the servant brought it. It was so hot that by the time it reached me the sound of ice was stilled. The *punka-wallah* began to fan me, standing behind the head of my bed, while across the veranda and away over the parched ground the heat danced thickly.

"*Khana tiyar, Huzoor* [Lunch is ready, your Honour]."

"Lunch? Oh, of course, but how can we have lunch when everything is packed?"

"Your Honour gave orders for the food to be brought from the hotel." It is the custom to keep one's own servants to cook one's food and not to employ those of the host.

Yes, but it was cool then. Strange how this heat goes to one's head. It must be like the effect of opium.

Curry! Who can eat curry with the thermometer at 100 in the shade, after seven months without a drop of rain? I cast a disgusted eye over the lunch-table and attacked a melon. The bearer received the benefit of my ire and my freely expressed opinion. The cook was sent for.

"What do you mean by serving a lunch like this on a hot day?"

Khansama said he had done his best with what the hotel kitchen provided. It would not occur again, he apologized—"for how could I, your Honour, do anything to displease you, who are my father and mother? And what is my lot in life but to serve your Honour?"

After all, I was too hot to be hungry. The heat was like a boiling blanket outside. The road was deserted. The Jumna river was dried up until only a narrow ribbony stream was visible. The rooms were suffocating. Even the electric fan only deluged me with hot air and shutting it off I called for more iced water.

One becomes as peevish as an infant in such an atmosphere.

My bearer now appeared to say the trouser-presses, riding-boots, and boot-trees were yet to be packed. But where?

"Put them in canvas and rope them up." Bright idea!

The *dhobi* (washerman) sent a message to say that as he had just buried his grandmother he could not deliver the laundry until the next afternoon.

Heavens! The laundry not arrived yet! This

was too much; the next afternoon we should be in the train well away from Delhi.

"Bring the *dhobi.*"

It was not his fault that his grandmother chose this time to pass, much less that there was not a hamper left in which to pack the clothes. He was all repentance after having been given a good talking to, such as would have caused a revolution in a trade union, and he promised to deliver the clothes that night.

Surely there was nothing forgotten now! Khansama appeared, worthy and greatly underestimated man, to say that if I had anything left over requiring a hamper, his wife's nephew's father-in-law could oblige with one.

Visions of heaps of laundry had just been rising before me demanding to be hampered. How thankful was I to hear of that hamper, but I did not let him see it.

Instead I replied, "Yes, there may be a few things. Ask this nep—er—relation to bring the hamper at once."

Congratulating myself on my organizing powers I settled down with a month-old English newspaper and had just read the 'home' weather report—"the wettest summer for twenty years"—when voices of unaccustomed loudness reached me intermingled with one apparently anxious to smooth matters over. Suddenly some one rushed on to the veranda, his bare feet thudding on the carpet.

"Who is there?" I called hastily, thinking a servant had found a snake too near the bungalow.

The cook's mate (assistant) appeared, gingerly looking back as if pursued, and could only speak two words:

"The money-lender!"

"The what?"

"The *bunia*, your Honour. He gave me three rupees for my sister's wedding and now ten want. I not got. He got *lathi* [long heavy stick], *badmash* [bad man]. He kill me, Huzoor."

"Tell him to come later."

"He say he sit till he get."

Knowing the Hindu money-lender's creed and not caring for any more side-lines in an already over-crowded show, and feeling the business of looking after the servant was as much my affair as the rupee-gathering was the *bunia's*, I gave him ten rupees on condition he borrowed no more from the Shylock of the bazaar. The promise was readily given and probably as readily forgotten.

I again applied myself to the newspaper. Another vicious argument was now in progress outside the drawing-room. The voices were not high-pitched, it was true, but the knife-edged words were disconnected. As the number of voices increased I thought it was time for direct interference, and, being slightly worked up by the heat and prevailing conditions of general disorder, I forgot my unseemly Western haste and precipitated myself almost in the midst of the wordy combat. My knowledge of Hindustani was at that time very limited. So I called a halt. Five pairs of eyes were glaring furiously upon a perspiring bearer, the man we had sent to the station for the coats. Singling him out I asked if my order had been obeyed. He replied in English:

"Six trunks all alike, Huzoor. Which one coat wanted, how I know?"

This was quite right, but the others imagined his intuition ought to have guided him to the right one.

Here was another puzzle! Another bearer offered to go and do the best he could—while Khansama, thinking that a pillar which hid him also deadened the voice, called "Son of a——" (something my two months' vocabulary did not contain).

The coats were brought at a late hour as I was explaining to the cook the details of the lunch hampers to be ready by 7 A.M. sharp, the time we had to leave for the station. The hamper of the cook's nephew's father-in-law stood open, ready for the laundry which at that moment put in an appearance, as the *dhobi*, perched on the top of the bundle, rode his donkey into the servants' quarters. As the washing was twice the size of the donkey, one would have thought it had enough to contend with, instead of having its master as well. I gave the washerman eight rupees (his pay for a whole month's washing), and the last hamper was packed. The next morning Margaret and her *ayah*, Syed and I, were packed into the car while the servants and the luggage were loaded into five *gharis*. Just as we were leaving the bungalow a figure raced across the yard literally hung with kettles, pots, lids, pans. It was Khansama, who lived in great fear of leaving anything behind. Taking farewell of our host we left for the station.

The station was a mass of humanity, servants, *ayahs*, children, babies, and dogs. I sought out a station official and had a carriage reserved for the journey and our luggage weighed. Had not this precaution been taken we might have been standing there until the next day, but the power of ten shillings oiled the wheels. By the time all the porters and guards had told their stories of how they had achieved the impossible by getting the servants into the overcrowded train and our luggage into the vans, it had cost us nearly five pounds.

Khansama was to be seen still draped in the articles associated with his calling, trying to find room in the servants' compartments where he might not be too unwelcome. An application to the guard and another five shillings got him in. When he saw the money the guard assured me he had been trying all the time to get a place for my cook in keeping with my dignity! Who could show displeasure after such diplomacy?

On came the travellers until the train was packed. Our compartment, being reserved and occupied by only my husband and myself, had many vacant seats.

The vendors were calling:

"Melons! Bananas! English sweets! English newspapers! Sacred water for Hindus only! Water for Muslims only! Lemon sherbet for everybody!"

The raucous cries became deafening as the train was about to leave and the prey to escape! The people who could not get seats were running up and down. Unable to stand it any longer I opened our door and removed the "Reserved" label. There was a concentrated rush. It was the 'survival of the fittest,' and the compartment was soon full. A giant Pathan sat down just opposite. We exchanged the usual "*Salaam alaikum*," or Muslim salutations, just as the Hindu with the earthenware jar of sacred water for Hindus only passed the door.

"*Pani! Pani!* [Water! Water!]" he called monotonously. The word made the Pathan jump to his feet. He called the water-carrier back, but as soon as the man saw the would-be purchaser, he became exceedingly humble, and not a little agitated: for the Pathan was of Muslim faith, and if he so much as touched the vessel containing the water it would be polluted and useless for any Hindu.

"*Wai*, son of a mad father, bring the water," shouted the Pathan.

Still cringing reluctance showed largely in the attitude of the Hindu. Waiting for no more, the Pathan jumped from the carriage and, raining blows on the unfortunate upholder of his faith, spat twice into the sacred water.

"Go now, son of a jungle cat, and sell thy water. I will not detain thee." No one took any notice of the incident; a policeman on the platform was lost in the bliss of orange-sucking.

Fire danced in the eyes of this son of the Khyber—the glint of defiance one never sees anywhere in India. Sitting down opposite me he began to eat mangoes—not as we eat them, but by bursting the top and sucking the sweetness. There is no doubt this is the most efficient way, but it is not one to be adopted for general use—if one wants to be popular!

We were away at last from the Capital. The Jumna with its dancing haze was soon left far behind. The grilling in the Plains of unending flatness had started. The sun streamed unmercifully into our carriage. A slight manipulation of those set-of-three windows gave us air, and darkened the compartment. The electric fan did noble duty. The Pathan had now started on melons. Yes, I ruminated, certainly the mangoes were an improvement, but then it is said one must eat a melon noisily to get the full flavour; our fellow-traveller appreciated flavour.

The other occupants of the carriage seemed still to be enjoying the peace which descends after a rush of more than ordinary acuteness. The pale little man with eyes closed, in the opposite corner beside his large florid wife—at least, I guessed she was his wife by the masterful way she took charge of him—was certainly not going to enjoy the train. He already showed all signs common to the bad traveller, and slightly trying to those who feel more or less at home in such circumstances. He was in capable hands in any case.

The thinnest of coats now began to be cast off. Brows were mopped. The Pathan sang snatches of warlike songs. So little notice did he take of us that we simply did not exist for him. At the sound, a look of pain shrivelled the little man's face, and his robust wife showed signs of rebellion as she glanced meaningly in the direction of the singer. Her white topee might have grown on her head, so definitely and defiantly was it mounted there. She plied her ailing husband with water, a damp handkerchief, smelling salts; but he was well beyond caring about these.

On rattled our train through miles of sugar-cane, stretches upon stretches of land which seemed to belong to nobody, vast open lifeless spaces—until we lost interest in outside things and prepared for a stop at Saharanpur.

Those of us who were lucky enough to have sufficient will-power and 'personality' had slept fitfully. Saharanpur is a very large station and a perfect paradise for vendors of practically anything. It is not every one who cares to get out of bed and bargain for brassware, carpets, or woodwork in the early hours of the morning. Yet the place was alive with the sellers of all these commodities as well as fruit, tea, sweets, biscuits, lemonade, soft drinks and even carved tea-tables. How the quiet figures lying on the platform wrapped in the blankets slept on through the din passes my comprehension.

The platform was buzzing with our fellow-travellers anxious to refresh themselves. A journey is *tamasha* (fun), for all travellers in India. Friends greeted each other affectionately, servants stood hand in hand enjoying every minute in the rabble, while the sellers of the various allurements were amply recompensed for having lost their rest.

Everybody was eating, but the talking went on just the same.

"All in now!" and the scramble began afresh. Servants snatched at the fruit of the unwary and jumped into the moving train, waving to the losers an invitation to come for the money.

We settled down again, for this was the last stop before Kalka at the foot of the Simla hills. Here we arrived in time for lunch and rejoiced at the sight of the towering hills, the fresh green of the grass and trees, the smell of pure air. It was a small station where one could get lunch either in the little shack a few yards up the hill or brought to the compartment. Here, too, we changed to the train which was to take us up the eight thousand feet. If it is a first journey, as it was mine, one takes a good lunch and looks forward to the joy of climbing the hill. The meal is not a long affair and I was soon in the hill-train. Not so crowded this time.

Two seats only. Our pale little man and his wife with the still resolute topee were with us again, opposite as before. Calm resignation in the face of long odds sat on the face of the long-suffering one. He was still in the grips of *mal-de-chemin*—still plied with water he did not want, and frequent applications of wet handkerchiefs from his strong-minded companion. Thinking he must be a poor specimen at best, I turned to the window to get a full view of the welcome hills.

We were off. Looking down from the window on one side into grassy depths and away up into green heights on the other, it felt good to be alive, to see the hills again. There came a blast from the engine. A tunnel!

"Are there tunnels?"

"Yes, ninety-nine," some one volunteered.

"How thrilling!" Green grassy depths, green grassy heights, and tunnels after the parched, brown, shrivelled plains. We seemed to be going round. The sun was not hot now, only warm and pleasant. We opened the window. Another deafening shriek. Of course a tunnel, but how the train rattled! Round again, and then the green depths became deeper. A narrow road like a pale withered serpent wound far below. The moving dots on it were cars of those who preferred the road journey up the hill—those who knew the ninety-nine tunnels! It seemed a stupid idea, still, round again, another tunnel—this circular movement made me feel a little uncomfortable, almost like being on a rough sea. It must have been the effect of looking down. Silly to do so, but it was wonderfully fascinating to watch the depth grow. Yes, that sick feeling would be difficult to get rid of. I pitied the poor pale little man who seemed to be experiencing it too. Perhaps the nausea would soon pass. It did not pass. It increased. That corkscrew railway was not the fun it promised to be. The whistling, rattling train made my head ache. I leaned out of the window to get the cool air. The depths were giddy—I wished I could roll out of that labouring shrieking contraption into the peace and coolness of that unending greenness. The little man was now at grips with the same feeling. I offered the Trojan a cushion for him and sat down again, leaning on the window, head on arm.

Great high trees of rhododendrons were almost within reach, but they were no joy to me. We became talkative and sympathetic towards each other. We relaxed, all but the large woman in the topee. She irritated me terribly, and I lay on the other arm so that her face was away from my sight.

"The last tunnel, the ninety-ninth," said some conscientious person comfortingly. It was over! With a rasping jolt we came to a stop. Strange how soon the excitement revived me! The station was commonplace—the hills closed us in. It was very cold and bleak. With much difficulty and the passing of many more rupees, we got outside with our luggage, wrapped in our fur coats. It seemed our troubles were not over. Lines of rickshaws quickly drew away, as the first experienced travellers packed into them. Turbaned rickshaw coolies, bare-legged and barefoot, with coarse blankets round their bodies, vied with each other for one's patronage.

"Here, here, memsahib, nice good seats! Carry memsahib quick," they yelled.

In we got, and the four men, two in front and two at the back, began to pull and push us up the steep hill out of the station. It was terribly cold there for us from the Plains. The hills had an enchantment which we had forgotten. The pine- and deodar-trees sparkled in the cold sunlight. We drew the exhilarating air deep into our lungs. Up and up we went to the grunting of the coolies as they mounted panting, for the hills are sometimes almost

A Tribal Gathering of Pathans

perpendicular. At last we came to the shops, which were preparing for 'the season' and were all well stocked and attractive. Past the post office and along through the hills. Now the road was level, the feet of our rickshaw men thudded as they flew with us over the hard road, not dusty like the roads of the Plains.

Now the road fell away to a giddy depth. Surely we would have to walk here! But no, we went hurtling down. There was no fence on the left where the ground fell away in a precipice. We skimmed past the wicked-looking valley round a corner at a pace which made me grip the sides of the rickshaw in trembling fear. Away across the valley the hills rose again, dotted with tin-roofed bungalows. There up on the right-hand side was our hotel.

I had seen nothing more beautiful than the view from the hotel—deep woods, rising verdant hills, and away behind it all, like the frosted ice on a Christmas cake, sparkled the breath-taking snow-clad Himalayas, against a sky of deep blue.

We spent a few weeks in the hotel until our bungalow, where we were to spend some months, was put in readiness. We had three rooms, dined in the hotel dining-room, and, as there was no lounge, invited our acquaintances after the ceremony of card-leaving—they are sticklers for cards in India—to our own rooms. There was as in all hotels an amusing collection of visitors. At table our right-hand neighbour was an old colonel who swore from 5 A.M. until dinner-time at night, after which he completely lost the power of speech, but acquired the compensatory gift of snoring. On our left sat the dear old mother of many sons, a distinguished soldier's widow whose husband came out in the 'sixties with those rare English gentlemen who really desired to serve India. She knew everybody who had ever been anybody for the last fifty years. One day I spoke admiringly of a famous general.

"Oh, him! I knew him when he was a lieutenant. I've smacked his ears too! They needed it!"

It was she who, on hearing that a young countrywoman of hers was drinking too much, threatened her with a horse-whipping. Would there were more of her type in high places to-day in unhappy India!

A tea-planter who could tell audacious stories and make people believe them was our neighbour overhead. He talked loudly and sweepingly about 'home,' although it was obvious to many that it was not his birthplace. He once told me, in a burst of confidence, that his grandfather belonged to 'home' and had settled in Ceylon. He usually applauded any conversation dealing with England by saying with a swift intake of breath through his teeth, "That's the place!"

A pale clerk who never forgot to remind us he was "predestined for the I.C.S." was another amusing fellow-diner. As soon as a new 'brass-hat' arrived, he at once sent cards and usually left those sent in return where everybody could see them. He would ask if anybody had noticed a belonging of his anywhere. When asked what it was, he replied, "Only a card from my dear old friend

Brigadier-General——" or "Lord——, so good of him to let me know of his arrival. Of course, these people know about me." I presume he referred to the predestined affair. They evidently knew too much to invite him anywhere, all the same.

We were more than faintly interested when one night a picturesque diner occupied a whole table to himself. He wore long hair, a large schoolgirl bow of black velvet ribbon at his neck, and a monocle. Hushed murmurs went round. "A famous artist!" "English?" "Oh, yes, travelling incognito to get new types for his Royal Academy picture!" He left cards on us all and we laughed, for we thought it a ruse, although who started the story was not established. People are inclined to take a portion of salt where a celebrity is concerned; it is generally required in the East in such circumstances. Whether we imagined ourselves decorating the honoured walls of the Royal Academy or were simply interested in art I do not know, but before long four of us were committed to canvas. Did we think the likenesses good? Personally we were slightly disappointed in our own, but then we always are, and the others were really marvellous. Not only was our artist a portrait-painter, but a very Landseer into the bargain. He roamed about a good deal and if he saw a dog worthy of his brush he sent his card to the owner and asked permission to paint the pet. He appeared to be a lonely man, with no relations, and not very talkative.

By this time we had left the hotel for our little house down on the hill-side. What a joy those hills were again after the unending Plains! Our artist sent my portrait, asking if we would care to have it. Assuming it to be a gift I wrote accepting it with suitable thanks. A few days later the bill came. It was not for a large sum as paintings go, but it was the total lack of modesty on the part of the artist that annoyed me and made me return the picture. Later I found that everybody else had had the same experience and that some of the dog-owners had paid up. The response to his appeals, I heard, were less than a quarter of what he had expected and this meant he must have had to take—when he left Simla suddenly—a goodly collection of pictures in which strangers would not be particularly interested.

Picnics were organized and we set out in full force, scrambling down into the valleys. As was only to be expected this did not meet with the approval of all. For instance, the fat lady from Calcutta refused to see the fun in what we enjoyed and sat down on the side of the hill-track, where she remained without any tea until we returned home hours later.

Jacko Hill was a favourite spot for visitors who were interested in the multitude of monkeys to be seen there. Many years ago an English boy who had attended school near the monkey hill had become so attached to the place that when he grew up he renounced everything and went back to Jacko Hill to live. He fed the monkeys and taught them to come when he called them by name. The chief monkey, Rajah, was the leader and never gave precedence to any of the others.

One day some friends and I climbed this hill. More than half-way up we came on a line of monkeys drawn up right across our path. We had brought bread for them, and I was carrying a loaf under my arm. Before we knew what had happened, the biggest monkey sprang at me, seized the loaf and tore it up, distributing it as he thought fit. That finished, they began to creep stealthily down upon us, while we thought it wiser to retreat, fearing every minute they would leap upon us. We had gone up the wrong side of the hill and they resented the intrusion, and followed us right down within sight of our picnic things. That was my last pilgrimage to the monkey hill.

CHAPTER XVII

THE HINDU MARRIAGE FAIR

"*SALAAM, HUZOOR*," said my *ayah* one morning. "Spare me to-day, Sipi Fair day."

"You always say you are too old for enjoyment, Ayah, and you cannot keep away from a hill fair," I replied.

"Nay, Huzoor, I am old, but have two daughters. To-morrow I get husbands for them—you know, at the marriage market."

I kept silent.

"Very good husbands at hill fair. My own husband hill-fair man," said Ayah with dreamy reminiscence.

"All right, then go for the day."

"Thank you. *Salaam, Huzoor!*"

Still Ayah lingered. "Huzoor giving me some pay before? Five, six rupees, Huzoor?"

"All right," I replied shortly.

"May Sahib one day be the Laut-Sahib [Viceroy]!"

"Khansama," I said as that worthy came for orders, "remember to-morrow morning breakfast will be at eight sharp. I am going *shikar*."

The cook's ready answer was not given as usual, and I looked to where his toe dug in an embarrassed way into the earth.

"Huzoor," he faltered, "to-morrow my daughter get husband . . . if . . ."

Heavens! Another projected marriage! Then I remembered.

"Oh, you mean the hill fair. You want to go?"

"Yes, Huzoor, me poor man, Huzoor. Memsahib giving me five, six rupees?"

For the second time I hesitated and was lost.

The day dawned and the early sun jewelled the deodar-trees and away up in the branches the monkeys chattered. Breakfast for once was on time—my least desire was a sacred command. Every servant was within sight, displaying the anxiety common when expectations threaten to fall short.

"Come here, all of you," I called, and in a flash the entire staff was at attention a few feet away.

"Do you all want to go to the fair?" The smiles and sidelong looks at each other answered before they did. "Very well, here are five rupees each *baksheesh*, but don't bring any wives here!"

Five minutes later, chattering like jackdaws, they were off down the hill. The morning sun glinted on the silver of Ayah's nose and earrings and heightened the bright colours of the men's turbans. Ayah was not a stranger to the fair, for she had six nose-rings—a ring for each husband (not all at the same time). Interested in the variegated colour of their clothes, I failed to notice the appearance of my *shikari*. My gaze lingered on him in partial recognition. This mauve turban and bright coat were surely not for the chase—yet he had turned up no doubt trusting to my soft-heartedness.

"*Salaam, Huzoor!*"

"A good day for *shikar*," I remarked in a business-like way, taking no evident notice of his garb. Intuition, however, told me that the news of the exodus from my bungalow to the fair had spread.

My remark caused a look of anguish on the man's face. It seemed poor sport to tease him, so in another minute he was racing down the hill to join the throng. Every hill road was alive with colours that would have made a peacock jealous. Snatches of lilting songs were borne to me across the valley. Surely every woman for twenty miles wanted a husband!

I too had become infected with the germ, and within half an hour was one of the throng. All roads that day seemed to lead to the marriage market.

By and by we came to a narrow goat-track. The hills appeared a strange place for such a gathering until we came on the scene itself. Then it seemed that this hill background was the most suitable in the world. It was worth while to come any distance to see these light-hearted *Paharis* (hill-people). There were booths of every kind, sweetmeats, fruit, caps, shawls, slippers—a veritable shopland had found its way along the winding hill-tracks.

In front of me sat a man with matted hair wearing nothing save a loincloth. Half beggar, half saint, he was greatly feared, for it was said his prayers were always answered. Therefore the gift of a few annas in order that he might say a good word for you was preferable to giving him nothing and imagining things.

Over there sat the charm-seller who was known to have direct communication with Shaitan, who feared him greatly—so that again a few annas for a charm, however ineffective, brought peace of mind. What were these things in bottles? Spirits. What kind? Methylated? No, evil spirits! This was scarcely comforting as no doubt the old saint-like exhibitor had discovered to his advantage.

For six annas it was possible to have any evil spirit that might happen to be floating round captured and put in the bottle. It was cheap for a rupee to have the couple he found round me bottled!

Holding a tiny empty glass jar, he spoke quickly for half a minute, then filled the vessel with water-like liquid—some clever sleight of hand followed, because in less than a minute a perfect gargoyle was floating in the liquid. Shuddering, I handed him a rupee and turned away just as he caught sight of another. That being caught and safely screwed down, I left the poorer for two rupees but the richer for a prayer on my behalf, which, as I looked at the 'spirits,' made me feel was not ill spent.

"Tell fortune, memsahib, only eight annas. All truth."

I succumbed. The usual wealth was coming, a sea voyage safe to predict, and luck which took nearly three minutes to recite.

Then the enclosure of pretty girls. Surely this was the arena from whence the youths would choose their wives. All round circled the would-be husbands. It was not easy to choose if they sought beauty in a wife.

They wore no veils. Behind and on one side stood the fathers of the young men, while on the other were the girls' fathers. A few shy youths hung back but were pushed forward, blushing all over, to try their luck in the marriage game. Their bashfulness gave place to open-mouthed wonder, and once their interest was aroused they were soon in the crush for the front row.

The girls were enjoying the excitement and doing their bit to make up the young men's minds for them. Old men with henna-red beards, forgetful of the amusement they caused, pushed in, but the girls looked mockingly at them and laughed among themselves. Soon a youth beckoned to a pretty girl, who joined him outside the enclosure. At once two old men bore down on them—the fathers. Here was romance with a touch of business thrown in.

"My daughter," the old man was saying, "has much beauty, therefore her dowry will not be so large."

Judging by the eyes of the two as they gazed at each other the dowry was not of great moment.

"One cow, two goats, two bags of flour," the girl's father went on, "and a hundred rupees in silver coins."

"Two cows," parried the boy's father, "two cows had she been plain, but as she is beautiful I had thought only of the goats—but having only two daughters I am giving each a cow over and above."

"So let it be, then."

The pact met with the elders' approval, and the handsome couple led the way to the sweet-stall, followed by the fathers. The romance unfolding before my eyes gripped me, and I followed at a distance, entering into the spirit of the fun. "*Mithai* [sweets]," called the old sweet-seller, "sweets for pretty maidens! Sweets for beauty and delights of the eye!" The two young lovers stopped, hand in hand.

"Two rupees' worth of sweets," the boy said with careless abandon. With the stall-holder's blessing they passed on.

"Charms to ward off the evil eye?"

Ah, that appealed to them both! They each had one at eight annas. Again the boy paid. This after all was his day of days, and the hard-saved money and the weary hours of toil to make it were forgotten.

Long-life charms were selling vigorously, for what boy or girl did not want to live through many years with every day as happy as to-day!

Hundreds of pairs of young happy people descended on the booths. Gifts were bought and exchanged. The girls, having gained courage, presented their sweethearts to other girl friends who in turn introduced theirs. Healths were drunk in lemonade and sherbet. Then the young people danced while the elders discussed the business of the day.

"What was your Raisham's dowry?" "Yes, he is a fine young man," were expressions to be heard everywhere. I saw a handsome old woman with seven nose-rings, signifying that she had had seven husbands! Cheap, pretty coloured glass bracelets tinkled on every wrist and the old bracelet-seller who said he had had three wives during twenty years at this same market smiled reminiscently. "All beautiful girls with good dowries. Next year I might try again. The gods know best!"

The slanting rays of the sun and the chilly evening air saw the trek homewards. Lovers stood long, unwilling to part, waving again and again to each other as their less romantically inclined fathers struck out for home. There was music all along the road. In front of me on the path leading to my bungalow on the hill, in single file trekked my staff, all carrying bundles, happy and laughing. Judging by Ayah's excited conversation, she had done well for the daughters. They stood up to laugh loudly, reminiscently. Poor simple lovable folk, to-morrow will see them again on the treadmill, back to their stone-breaking, grass-cutting, housework! To-day at least they have 'lived'!

CHAPTER XVIII

EPISODES IN SIMLA AND DELHI

WE lay down for our afternoon siesta. A few hours later we awoke. How dull it looked, yet it was only four o'clock in the afternoon—slightly cooler too. We went to the veranda. The whole sky was overcast, a slight shivering as of fear passed occasionally through the trees. We could not tear ourselves away. Suddenly there was a tremendous crash. Thunder! Again it came, reverberating through the hills like the repeated detonation of a cannon. Long tongues of lightning stabbed the sky, reminiscent of the ribbon streamers thrown at a party. The monkeys began to chatter excitedly. Rickshaw coolies stopped a few seconds to throw split sacks round their heads and over their shoulders before dashing wildly to shelter.

The air was charged with electricity. I heard my hair crackling as the growing coolness made me smooth it back from my damp forehead. A few drops of rain fell on my upturned face, then a few more, a waft of cool June air passed caressingly over my forehead. Another deafening peal of thunder. Terrified at the suddenness, I rushed indoors just as the sound as of millions of pebbles crashed on to the tin roof of my bungalow. Rain at last! The monsoon!

The rain was awe-inspiring. Down it came steadily like a solid sheet of water. As if by the touch of a fairy wand a thousand little rivulets raced tumbling down the hill-sides. Water streamed everywhere; even the earth parched with months of gruelling heat could not cope with it. The monkeys rushed for safety into my veranda, where their primitive ideas made it certain that they would have the place to themselves. The noise on the tin roof lessened and finally stopped. There was only the gentle drip, drip, of the rain from the overhanging trees. Magically the sun burst out again. The beauty of a new world surrounded me. The dust had completely vanished from the winding road through the hills, and the sun as it struck the newly washed stones made them gleam and glisten. The roofs of the surrounding bungalows reflected the rays like looking-glasses. The deodar-trees trembled with diamond drops, their original freshness revived.

It was too wonderful to stay indoors. Tripping excitedly down the steep narrow path leading to the road, I hailed a passing rickshaw. "To the Library," I directed the coolies. "Go slowly." There was no dust from under the feet of the men in front. I breathed deeply the fresh air, and the new sound of iron striking the long-hidden stones as a pony galloped along towards me was a pleasure.

But why were the rickshaw men wrapping up their heads and shoulders? I had scarcely noticed that the sun had disappeared again—the sky was overcast, the coolies galloped along the road as the wind rose, and almost without warning down came the second torrent. Under the hood of my rickshaw I was safe from the downpour, and reached the Library as the storm burst furiously. Monkeys were shrieking and darting for shelter. Once inside, I stood by the window, from which point of vantage the pageant of unlucky ones was at its best or worst! That dusky European belle must have regretted her rashness when she saw her frillies drowned and felt the rain streaming from her hat which flopped unromantically round her shoulders. Would that poor friend, never a runner at the best, ever manage to reach shelter as she clung desperately to her soaking sunshade? I drew back from the window lest she should see me laughing.

A good deal of time was spent at the Library, a worthy building. The attraction of the English newspaper proved strong; we felt as we scanned the columns of *The Times*, albeit over a fortnight old, that we were once again in the midst of things and people that mattered, yet I wondered whether the Duchess of Blankshire, who, according to the Court Circular, gave a dinner-party at which the guests included . . . (here followed the names of all the *bon ton*), really felt the weight of her position half as much as did the Government official's wife who gave the party here yesterday. The odds were against the Duchess, for India—the historic land of unparalleled beauty—is still a land of slavery, where the fetishes of etiquette and class snobbery rule despotically and are worshipped by fanatical devotees.

I set out again to do some shopping.

"Go to Bachi Lal's shop," I said to the rickshaw men. Here I bought wool at nearly half the price it would have cost in the imposing-looking English shop over the way.

"Come see my fruit, memsahib," volunteered a fat man from where he sat cross-legged in front of his shop—his shoes lay beside him, and a rosary was in his hand.

"How much are your mangoes?"

"Four for one rupee. Very good Bombay mangoes."

"Too much," I argued, preparing to pass on.

"Six, then, for one rupee."

I hesitated. "No, I shall wait until they are cheaper."

"Memsahib, I am poor man, but will not refuse any English lady. What you give?"

"A rupee for a dozen."

"Very well, Huzoor. Boy, put a dozen mangoes in the Memsahib's rickshaw."

My purchases were finished, and as my rickshaw turned back through the bazaar the fruit-seller was slipping the beads of the rosary through his fingers as he voiced the ninety-nine attributes to Allah. Prayer was prayer, but then business was business.

"Hurry home," I said to the men. The time was getting nearer and nearer to dinner and I had a good way to go. At the top of the hill as we turned into the main road a khaki-clad policeman stopped the rickshaw.

"What is the matter?" I asked as I saw a line of rickshaws and people on horseback standing by.

"The Laut-Sahib and Bibi-Sahib [the Viceroy and Vicereine] are coming. All stop for the Laut-Sahib!"

"But I have only to cross the road to get into the one leading to my bungalow. There is nobody even in sight," I protested.

"My orders, memsahib," he said with emphasis.

The orders were given by my own countrymen, and the policeman had to keep his job, so I kept silent for half an hour, contrasting the simplicity of the Emperor of India's drives in London with the ceremony accorded to his representative in India itself.

It is true that there is in India no fence of barbed wire between the English people who matter and those who do not, but there might well be, for the cleavage is deep enough.

"What a clever woman Mrs—— is," I said one day to the wife of a high English official, as a gifted woman passed us in a restaurant.

"She might have been if her husband had been an I.C.S. man," she replied condescendingly.

"Do you know her? She has travelled round the world and is a very good speaker," I went on, anxious to bring out the highlights in my friend.

"No. You see, I am I.C.S. We have to be careful of our acquaintances."

Being conscious of the speaker's drab personality, the self-assurance and empty pride she gathered round her regarding her position, I understood the "I.C.S. ladies' sofa" in the club on the Plains, for I had unknowingly transgressed the rigid rules of etiquette and was for at least two minutes the recipient of some of the rudest stares ever given to a woman. The ladies were unknown to me that day in the club on the Plains, but not for long.

"Come, darling," said one of the least prepossessing as they rose in a quintette, "here is Mrs ——"—another woman of similar appearance was entering the room—"she is one of us, you know." All the hate engendered by high position which discounts birth was in her voice. Mrs—— was known to me, and we bowed in acknowledgment as the quintette swept down on my sofa, which I evacuated, thinking they had mistaken me for somebody else. Not so, however; these female Alexanders were not practising for the first time upon me. There are too many people in the Capitals, Hills, and Plains, who fail to realize that their birth and breeding are mere useless bagatelles when they confront the barbed-wire entanglements surrounding that most insurmountable of glassy mountains, the I.C.S.

"A very big sahib," the rickshaw *wallahs* had said in awe to each other as we waited for the Viceroy to pass, but the Hindu *babus* who met me at home with messages requiring answers were discussing the same subject within my hearing.

"Now, see you, these English people rule us all, this our country, all money going with big sahibs in England when retiring. Day coming when no money keeping here, then sahibs not wanting staying."

I held my peace, but noted their point of view.

"Kashmiri brought rugs for Memsahib to see," said Ayah the next day as she held the grass curtain for me to pass through to the veranda. I was confronted with carving, embroidery, jewellery, and deep blue turquoise boxes, all of beautiful workmanship. Nothing was priced—there is no such crudity.

"How much is that shawl?"

"Lady Sahib, that is the finest Kashmir ring shawl, a hundred rupees."

"Too much. What is this one?"

"Eighty rupees."

"They look alike," I said, eyeing the two minutely.

"No, memsahib," spoke the quiet-voiced Kashmiri, "different quality."

The hesitation might have been my imagination.

"These gold-embroidered bags are pretty."

"Yes, Lady Sahib, and cheap—only twenty rupees."

"Your things are too expensive," Ayah said finally. "Many Kashmiri come here with cheaper things. Memsahib does not need any from you."

The hill-man was evidently accustomed to the Western women who lacked the bargaining instinct. He waved his hand as though removing existing obstacles as he said, "Memsahib have a good look, no hurry."

"I will give you ten rupees for a gold bag."

"Ten rupees not pay material, but first transaction, I give."

Now things began to look cheerful. A set of dessert mats at fifteen rupees fell to my hammer at five. The shawl of superior quality was mine for thirty, thanks to Ayah, who kept an imaginary rival well in front of our salesman's eyes.

The haggling had tired me, and I was having a few minutes' rest when the bearer brought a whole armful of fox, lynx, snow-leopard, and mink skins. For a brief moment I thought one of my ships must have come home.

"The Kashmiri's brother leave these for Mem-sahib to see."

No price dangled accusingly to stress my inability to buy, such as is the way in England. Stroking the beautiful pelts, I thought I even overheard the Kashmiri of the veranda directing the steps of his brother-in-trade to my bungalow. He was the first of a long line of 'brothers' who called upon me with alarming regularity whether I bought anything or not.

Loaded luggage rickshaws, bound for the station, began to pass the road at the foot of the hill. The down-hill trek had begun. It was the end of September. We needed fires now, and afternoon tea was a cosy meal once more.

It was only when we packed for the journey that we regretted the encouragement we had given to the different box *wallahs*, and we had to buy more trunks to hold our one-time bargains, which were beginning to prove expensive.

As we started along the hill road, we found that we were almost the last. That busy hotel was closed for the season, all those bungalows too. Even the high and mighty Service ladies had returned to their sofa in the Plains club. The place looked suddenly dreary like a deserted dance-hall, once alive with music and life. Two men came level with our rick-shaw and pantingly salaamed. What did they want? It appeared that the cook had borrowed some rupees, promising to return them next month, and it was only an hour ago they heard we were leaving to-day.

Now the cook knew quite well he would not be in Simla in a month's time. He also knew that it was a far cry from Simla to Delhi, but he certainly overlooked the fact that it was the business of the lender to keep an eye on his rupees. The cook was ahead and now probably at the station. I paid the five rupees and deducted that amount, to the amazement of the borrower, from his month's pay.

It was cool on our return to Delhi, like a beautiful autumn in England. How glorious the old palace of the Moghul Emperors looked! There is the veranda through whose white marble fretted door-way the one-time Emperor appeared to receive the homage of his kneeling subjects. If anything pre-vented the ruler from gracing the veranda with his presence, no work was done by anybody that day, for what good could result on a day so ill begun? All around was the beautiful garden of the old palace. There was, too, the marble bath where the Moghul beauties once sported. The sandy part near the palace was where the Jumna once flowed. Now it has receded some hundreds of yards.

I entered the hall of public audience, the Diwan-i-Khas. For a moment I imagined the golden-robed Emperor seated on his white marble throne. A poor man is brought before him, so that his case may be heard. The man explains that he cannot pay his rent, as his oxen have died and his crops have suffered. The Emperor does not hesitate. Time will be given. The pleader prostrates himself on the floor in humble gratitude. The next case is brought. Dreams! But many such scenes must have occurred in this hall of the wonderful pure white marble canopy.

We were overcome by the majesty of it even to-day as it stood empty and deserted. The marble is inlaid with gold. Cheap replicas of those precious stones which during the Mutiny were hacked out by the victory-drunken despoilers twinkle in the ceiling and walls. I imagined the hordes of the Persian invader Nadir Shah gloating over the gorgeous beauty of the Peacock Throne, encrusted with priceless diamonds, sapphires, pearls, and rubies, which he carried off.

Then suddenly I started from my dreaming as my eyes took in the beauty of the Pearl Mosque—Moti Musjid. The domes glint in their opalescent colourings, returning every caress of the sun, snow-white against the sapphire-blue sky. The golden spire scintillates in regal magnificence. It might be newly built, so perfect it looks, except that to-day there are no craftsmen left who could compose such a poem in marble.

The keeper of the mosque asked me to go in. I removed my shoes. How easy it was to pray here! My heart was full of awe and reverence as I stood where the feet of so many mighty monarchs of old

India had passed, and I sat for a while in the garden.

Half an hour later I mixed once more with the jarring noises of the outside world. A wicked-looking *ghari-wallah* had almost collided with my car; retrieving his galloping horse, he steered for the centre of the road, and all but dashed into a sacred bull. The policeman with his back to these stirring happenings was evidently directing the traffic of some monkeys chattering high in a near-by tree, beneath which sat a *sadu* (holy man) throwing grain to the chatterers. The *sadu* was practically naked and indescribably dirty. Round his neck were rows of brownish beads. His long matted hair hung in lumps about his neck. His face was covered with ashes, denoting humiliation. I felt glad to get away from him. He seemed infinitely less human than the monkeys.

Here then was Chandi Chowk (Silver Street). Fat, prosperous-looking Hindus, wearing round caps and loincloths sat in their tiny stalls selling sweets or grain. The sacred bulls of the Hindus walked always in the centre of the narrow road, fully aware that neither Muslim, Christian, nor Jew dare put a hand on them. That did not prevent me from longing desperately to do so. Behind these the bullock-carts lumbered. Invitations to inspect the goods were too numerous to consider even if I could have made out what they were. One shopkeeper bolder than the rest grasped the door-handle of the car. I would have accelerated and got clear—in London the man would have been arrested—but there are other ways of doing business than in England. I stopped, and before there was time to speak to the shopkeeper, my car was surrounded.

"Alms in the name of Bhagwan [the Hindu god]!" roared an old hypocrite I knew well. "Alms for the hungry!" "Alms so that we may not die!" "May the Sahib be the Viceroy!" "May your Honour live for ever." "May you have a hundred sons!" Emaciated faces, smallpox-pitted faces, faces eaten by disease, crowded round the windows. The shopkeeper, feeling that this was scarcely an advertisement for him, said a few words which probably contained the merest hint of a promise. The crowd drew back. I stepped out. The shopkeeper, caring for nothing but what I should buy, and now having achieved his desire, threatened the crowd with a stick. Not that that could add anything to their present misery. They grovelled for the coins I threw, kissed my shoes, called on all the saints to preserve me, and went in search of a new prey.

With a jingling of bells a gaily dressed man passed on horseback, with garlands of flowers hung round his neck. All the young men walking beside him were making merry, for this was a Hindu bridegroom on his way to the old Jain temple for his marriage ceremony.

I felt envious of the carriage of that poor woman carrying a large brass pot on her head. She might have been an empress instead of an 'untouchable.' Behind her three little fat babies ran to keep pace with her steps. She carried another astride her left hip. All were quite naked but for a little charm tied by a string round their necks to avert the evil eye. Very solemn they looked—even the small one to whom I gave a few annas did not relax, but saluted gravely, while his mother thanked me profusely.

The smell of *ghee* filled the air as I passed the stalls of the sweet-seller. Flies were in millions. Then I came upon a snake-charmer, carrying two baskets on a pole across his shoulders, the snakes in one, a mongoose in the other. For a few annas he showed us a fight to the death between the agile little ferret-like animal and a huge reptile. He made way ungraciously for a donkey loaded with washing and his master to boot. That brought me to where rice was being weighed out by a patient shopkeeper sitting cross-legged holding the scales in his hand. The apparatus consisted of a bar from the ends of which two flat dishes dangled. It was easy to see there was no inspector of weights and measures here! At the next shop two Pathans were bargaining with a fruit-seller. The voices rose as the hill-men named their price. The stall-holder pleaded poverty and begged mercy. The melons were too expensive and the hill-men were pushed for time. The parleying of the fruit-seller did not suit them. They took a melon each, threw down a coin, and passed on grasping their *lathis* the more tightly. The shop-keeper took the money, tested its genuineness between his teeth, and looked after the two with a scowl, dwelling upon words he would fain say but dare not. Three British Tommies rounded the corner taking up the whole road with their bicycles. One bumped into a basket of fruit and knocked it over.

"Silly fool," called Tommy, "can't you keep your —— old barrow out of the way?"

The owner salaamed and cringed, as he would before the Laut-Sahib himself. Tommy was a big man in some circles in India. This was one of them. Good-naturedly he threw a coin to the sufferer, who was gathering up the scattered fruit. It was all over in a minute. Tommy whistled to his dog, and they were out of sight in a few seconds. No wonder he was popular.

My car moved slowly as we passed through about a dozen monkeys. They jumped out of the way on to a wall and the branches of the trees. These were special animals who chose to live near the monkey temple built to them by the Hindus. It looked for all the world like a monkey hotel. I stopped a few minutes to watch their quaint ways. One old grey monkey was chattering away into the ear of another like himself. From time to time he pulled his head back to get a better view of the effect of his words on his friend. Another mother monkey was spring-cleaning her babies' heads—busily, I might add, but not so occupied as to be unable to give a resounding back-hander to a little one taking advantage of her occupation. A game of tail-catching was in progress in front of the temple. On the roof a contingent sat motionless, reminding me of the platform at Udaipur station where their brethren race to meet all incoming trains, jump on to the roofs of the carriages, and beg for eatables.

Sitting by the roadside a little farther on was a *sadu* of a different type from the one I have previously described. He wore a dress of Grecian style, and a cloth cap of the same stuff entirely covered his hair. His beard and moustache were not so dirty, nor was his face; he might, though, just have washed after many months. His right arm was held up, and had been so long in this position that he could not lower it. One can only hope the high spiritual achievement reputed to be reached in such a painful way was justified. His neighbour a little farther on across the road was free from religious scruples. Bareheaded he sat sheltered from the sun beside an array of tins and bottles of all sizes. Each one was labelled with the name of a cure. The tiniest bottle was priced at two rupees. Probably that was the price he thought I looked capable of paying, for I know my *ayah* paid four annas.

"Good certain cure for grey hairs."

That being of no interest to me for some considerable time, I hoped, I inquired what the green liquid was. Ah, that was the *pièce de résistance*!

"This," he cooed, taking the small bottle lovingly in his hand and stroking it, "this juice is gathered only at midnight, and is always found where cobras live." I shivered. "Two drops will turn the most beautiful woman into a witch."

This was a little unexpected. "Do you sell much of it?"

"Very much, most useful for second wives; husbands bring home!"

He grinned wickedly. Not believing greatly in the mixture, I handed him a few coins so as not to give him any desire to work on me any of the spells he vowed he was master of.

A black dancing bear appeared round the corner. His master looked capable of teaching him all the necessary tricks. I asked him how much he earned a day.

"Not enough to give myself food after the bear is fed," replied the rascal. The bear at once stood on its hind legs, clapping its paws. I gave the *tamasha-wallah* enough to get a meal for both of them, and the bear saluted and bowed its head. The dirty *sadu*, still sitting under the monkey tree, had been joined by half a dozen others like himself. Two in particular struck me. Their heads seemed to be covered with black snakes coiling down to the ground which proved to be tails of plaited hair. These fakirs worked strands of goats' and monkeys' hair into the plaits to achieve length. They sat silent, for speech was forbidden them lest it should give comfort, which, being earthly, was not permitted. The *sadu* who sat by the wayside near my bungalow was a professional beggar. His little brass bowl with the handle rested before him. He was desperately dirty and was supposed to be a magic-worker. None of my servants dared to pass him after dark, and, as a matter of fact, I myself would not have done so on foot.

He never moved his eyes, yet always seemed to be staring at you in an uncanny way. Once when I laughingly remarked about him to an old Delhi *ayah*, she took sweetmeats to the shrine of a saint to propitiate him in case my remarks had been heard by the magic-worker. Sitting on the veranda at my feet in my bungalow facing the Jumna, she told me the following tale within a hundred yards of where the hero of it sat.

Some years ago the fame of this fakir travelled far, and people came to him to work any magic they required. He would only take a few annas from a poor man, but from the rich he would only accept gold. His small lamp was kept alight with the oil taken from the heads of people luckless enough to be obliged to pass his way after midnight! In the Jumna live many crocodiles, and it was said he carried on conversations with them and gained much wisdom which he imparted to human beings in need of it. Crocodiles are unpopular. The fakir, however, lived in harmony with them and at nights if he required to cross the broad Jumna they formed a bridge and he passed over dry-footed. Be that as it may, the fakir often stood closer to them than most people dared.

One of these monsters, larger and uglier than the rest, was his special pet, and it was known that if the *sadu* did not visit him for a whole day the crocodile assumed the shape of an owl and flew to the tree under which the saint sat. This creature had eaten many women and children who had ventured too near the water, unaware of the danger lurking therein. No hunter had ever been able to bag Nazar, the great crocodile, who never had been known to try to escape his would-be assailants, and in time a price was set on his head and an old Cavalry colonel offered five hundred rupees to the officer who would kill the crocodile. It was known that when not under the influence of *sherab*, or the English wine, the Colonel was a quiet, efficient soldier, and one who did not encourage gambling in the lower ranks.

Thus Nazar, "the Light of the Jumna," went on his wicked way and flourished, greatly to the dismay and discomfort of those for whose relations' disappearance he was solely accountable. But as he was the magic-worker's possession, the poor people were unwilling to be drawn into conversation, lest it came to the ears of either the crocodile or the fakir, for any insult to his pet would be severely avenged.

A year passed, and still Nazar went free in spite of the Colonel's five hundred rupees; and still the fakir sat gazing in front of him at nothing in particular. Tales spread of his magic powers. The English made a joke of it, and said it was the ignorance of the uneducated servants. Nevertheless, they found it increasingly difficult to get servants to take any duty in the bungalows facing the Jumna. Servants would only speak in wide-eyed horror of the far-famed fakir, and each story beat its predecessor.

One day the fakir was alleged to have caused a Hindu woman who stared inquisitively at him to disappear into the ground. There was another tale of a dog that bit him, which he turned into a stone. He was said to have picked a cobra out of the path of a little Hindu boy whom he found crying and terrified in the jungle. Nobody had ever seen him cook a meal, for it was said the jungle spirits brought him all he required when he took his meal at midnight.

One day a party of English people were picnicking near, so ran another tale. They sent a servant with a rupee for the fakir. The children were throwing stones and nuts into the water. Suddenly there was a splash—a little girl had fallen in. The servants shrieked in terror. The only word one could make out was "Crocodile"! The next minute Nazar was approaching with open mouth. An old servant, heedless of the danger, threw himself into the water, swimming for the child who was almost within reach of the crocodile.

Everybody shrieked. There was little hope of the servant reaching the child in time, and, even if he did, it would be but to share the same fate.

Suddenly a ragged and dirty figure appeared. It was the fakir. He said a few words which nobody understood. The crocodile, whose great jaws were about to engulf the servant, unexpectedly turned away from its prey and swam back to the bank where the fakir stood.

Willing hands were now assisting the terrified servant and child to the safety of the dry land, while across the river the fakir was playfully throwing water over the crocodile. The fakir took no notice of the others, never raising his eyes from his pet.

Since that day neither Englishmen nor Indians have ever spoken ill of the fakir. The Colonel withdrew the five hundred rupees reward, and Nazar continues on his wicked way unharmed to this day.

Believe it or not, in such terms it was related to me.

CHAPTER XIX

EAST AND WEST

MY husband had accepted a Government post while we were in Simla, and for this reason we came back again to Delhi, where we were to remain for a month or so longer until we should return to the Frontier.

While in Delhi I received urgent news from Scotland. My mother's health was causing anxiety, and it was thought advisable for me to go home.

My father-in-law and the rest of the family were very grieved to know we were going so far away from them again, and many messages arrived before we left, begging us to come as soon as ever we could. Bonfires would always be waiting to celebrate our homecoming, they said, and they would not be happy until we were with them again.

We returned to Scotland, where Margaret was delighted with the strangeness of everything. She thought the house very small and wondered what would happen if there was a raid, as she saw no loopholes. She would suddenly call out at most awkward moments, "Mummy, where are these ladies' trousers?" or "Why has that man not got his gun?" Once when a devout minister came to tea with us Margaret was brought to see him. She arrived in the room just as the visitor was telling us how he had unsuccessfully tried to bring a delinquent to the right path. "Don't worry about him, Mr Cameron," she said. "Just send him to my grandfather, he'll deal with him for you!"

It seemed as strange to think of the 'Free Land' in the West as it was to visualize the West on the Frontier. In the West one becomes as a hot-house plant, which a waft of Frontier air would wither. One's brain whirls with the hectic bustle of the Western city. How, one wonders, do these people keep their reason in the midst of these endless shops? What life could be long enough to take advantage of all the amusements offered every day and within reach of the poorest?

I grudged the early morning hours everybody wasted at home. Nothing seemed to get going before nine o'clock, while beyond the Frontier and even in India we had done two or three hours' riding by then. People annoyed me by being surprised that I had been happy in the 'Free Land.' The majority had only heard of it in a remote sort of way. Some did know it was "somewhere near India," and one woman held up her hands in horror and asked whether all they said about witch-doctors was true! Others tactfully suggested that of course I would not be going back, or that I was lucky not to have been given ground glass in my food!

They hedged round the question as to whether my husband was a Christian; was I the only wife, and if so how was it he had not married in his cradle? A visitor assured me on good authority, her brother having been a missionary in China, that all these men were married many times, and if I would take her advice while there was yet time I would stay at home, where women were not chattels.

This latter word seems to apply in one all-embracing sweep to any woman outside the British Empire. Several times when these women used to gather round to hear 'harem stories' I often felt disposed to wander, for their benefit, in the realms of imagination. Another woman said, when no lurid tales were forthcoming, that she was sure the subject was a most painful one for me, and having been brought up as I had undoubtedly been she understood my reluctance to discuss it!

In India, I found feeling runs slightly high over these East and West marriages. The Englishwomen there resent their countrywomen marrying Indians, and I have been told that in many cases the lives of Englishwomen married to Indians have been made perfectly unbearable by the treatment and intolerance of the English colony. The Indians I found were kindly hospitable people, and I am confident that if Western wives who go to the East are prepared to treat the Easterns as equals, judge people by the goodness of their hearts, and not by the colour of their skins, there will be no problems to solve. On the other hand, the Indians can teach us much; if we would be less snobbish, it would be possible to see just what the Eastern culture is.

I learned the almost ideal law regarding woman's independence. This last sentence I have no doubt requires repetition. Please consider it repeated!

Every Indian and Pathan woman is provided for by dowry after she is married, and out of her father's income before. The fathers of these women would be ashamed to have their daughters earning their living. Moreover, when the father dies each daughter has her share of the estate. Added to this the daughters are given jewellery from time to time by members of the family so that they generally have a very considerable amount by the time they reach the marriage age. The thought of marrying without dowry and a fair supply of jewellery would never be entertained by Eastern girls. This custom completely does away with the feeling of being dependant on a husband, and one never hears of a young couple setting up house with scarcely more to their account than the four walls. Also a land-owner cannot sell any portion of his estate without his wife's permission. One can understand his reluctance to place himself in the position of being obliged to seek that consent four times over.

Since returning home I have discovered that the trouble in connection with these East and West marriages often begins in England. Hundreds of Eastern students from good families come to our universities. The people whose duty it is to consider their welfare seldom realize the obligation they have, with the result that these strangers fall a prey to a class they ought not to meet and would never know if they were introduced to the society they are perfectly capable of mixing with. Instead, however, they drift about, and the results have to be dealt with when the men return home qualified to take their places with any Westerner, but too often through an unfortunate Western marriage unable to do so. These instances happily are rare, but they exist.

The East is not a land of sweet-do-nothing inhabited by handsome, wealthy sheikhs lying in wait to lay hands on white women, load them with jewels, and loll away the sunny hours round lotus-ponds, fanned by great swarthy slaves practically naked. The same honest-to-goodness mode of living is required, the same decent standards of everyday life such as one associates with respectability must be observed in the East also, even if one has the money to live in regal luxury.

Having heard many stories in the Frontier land from travellers in India, I was forearmed as to what treatment would be meted out to me during my stay there. My surprise was great when the 'snob' community invited me everywhere. It may have been my husband's official position, or the fact, as one woman quite openly told me, that I was not the wife of an Indian! I must own the latter explanation was quite incomprehensible to me.

Life in India further taught me not to expect tolerance to be accorded to the ordinary Indian, and to see him treated as if he belonged to a servile race. On the other hand, I learned that the Frontier men are respected as an unconquered race.

It is not that this question of snobbery is unrealized by Westerners. I have had many opportunities for discussion, some of which I confess to having created with the object of adding to my collection of views! At a quite recent controversy with three women, wives of Service officials, I found their ideas in strange contrast. One of them said she was confident that a little give-and-take was the happy medium. The second, a lady with a title—which is a tremendous aid to prestige in India—said she preferred to remember she belonged to the ruling class, which must make itself felt. The third said she had always treated the Indians with respect, and had invariably found them courteous and quite intelligent. Lady number two who was one of those who took all but gave nothing, said she could never forget she was an Englishwoman, which is probably as well, because with her ideas it would not be so easy to be anything else.

Christianity seems to have spread among the 'untouchables' of India, that great army of the lowest class which the high-class Hindus scarcely consider human. It takes but the shadow of one of these unfortunates falling across a Hindu's cooking to render the entire food of a Hindu household polluted. No wonder, then, that the plank of Christianity, thrown as it is into the sea of misery in which these unwanted classes wallow, should be clung to so tenaciously. Yet this plank, while perhaps supporting life, is destined never to reach the shore. As each one becomes a Christian he or she is taught to believe that the conversion raises them to equality with the sahibs and memsahibs, because they are henceforth all brothers and sisters. Yet these classes after their acceptance of Christianity can at best become but step-brothers and step-sisters of the other Christians.

For generations they have been the sweepers in India, have been compelled by the Hindus to run out of sight when the latter are seen to approach, and are given food only if they leave their tin bowls right away from the proximity of the kitchens.

I made a point of talking—at a considerable distance—to women of this community of Christians, and found them very earnest in the belief that Jesus would give them whatever they prayed for; that when attired in their red flannel petticoats, antiquated white blouses, and solar topees, they were really memsahibs. But I noticed the old cringing servility inborn in the many generations; the fear of the Hindus and the important sahibs and memsahibs still remained, and will remain, as a scar is left after a wound. I wondered whether this religion that was new to them was doing good only for a part of their lives—the part when they donned their 'English' clothes and visited the Mission. If that were so, I reasoned, there was something wrong, something which to an onlooker like myself did not seem quite fair. It may still be but the first step in the right direction, or even the crawling towards that first step on their road to salvation.

My home in the near future will again be among people of a different race, in a land where life is simple and the honour of one's clan comes before anything else. It seems a plain straight-forward code, and ought to fit glove-like every race and every creed.

Travel-experiences prove that the East is no more lurid than the West. It should be no more difficult to impart this truth to people in this country than it was to me to point out the quite tractable ways of Westerners to the people of the Frontier.

Some day, perhaps long after the bonfires welcoming us back to the 'Free Land' beyond the Khyber have blazed and died, other bonfires may proclaim, even as our beloved poet Robert Burns so gloriously worded it, "Man to man the world o'er shall brothers be."

May it be so! *Inshaallah*—if Allah wills!

Printed in the United States
1299700002B/64